D0953125

DUSK, NIGHT, DAWN

RIVERHEAD BOOKS

NEW YORK

2021

DUSK, NIGHT, DAWN

On Revival and Courage

+

Anne Lamott

Riverhead Books
An imprint of Penguin Random House LLC
penguinrandomhouse.com

Grateful acknowledgment is made for permission to
reprint the following:

"Hymn to Time" first appeared in *Late in the Day* by Ursula
K. Le Guin, published by PM Press in 2015. Copyright © 2015 by
Ursula K. Le Guin. Reprinted by permission of Curtis Brown, Ltd.

Library of Congress Cataloging-in-Publication Data

Names: Lamott, Anne, author.
Title: Dusk, night, dawn : on revival and courage / Anne Lamott.
Description: New York : Riverhead Books, 2021.
Identifiers: LCCN 2020014324 (print) | LCCN 2020014325 (ebook) |
ISBN 9780593189696 (hardcover) | ISBN 9780593189702 (ebook)
Subjects: LCSH: Lamott, Anne. | Novelists, American--20th
century--Biography. | Christian biography--United States. | Faith.
Classification: LCC PS3562.A4645 Z46 2021 (print) |
LCC PS3562.A4645 (ebook) | DDC 813/.54 [B]--dc23
LC record available at https://lccn.loc.gov/2020014324
LC ebook record available at https://lccn.loc.gov/2020014325

Printed in the United States of America
1 3 5 7 9 10 8 6 4 2

Book design by Amanda Dewey

For Bill and Em

CONTENTS

Hymn to Time

Time says "Let there be"
every moment and instantly
there is space and the radiance
of each bright galaxy.

And eyes beholding radiance.
And the gnats' flickering dance.
And the seas' expanse.
And death, and chance.

Time makes room
for going and coming home
and in time's womb
begins all ending.

Time is being and being
time, it is all one thing,
the shining, the seeing,
the dark abounding.

• *Ursula K. Le Guin*

DUSK, NIGHT, DAWN

PROLOGUE:
RIBBONS

Here we are, older, scared, numb on some days, enraged on others, with even less trust than we had a year ago. The devastating pandemic, and the federal government's confused and deadly response, was simply the final straw to a few years of crushing developments. A UN report on climate catastrophe was published months before my wedding in 2019, the report of the extinction of one million species three weeks after. Major buzzkill. Our poor country has been torn asunder. I await the rain of frogs. And I've gotten so much less young. I got Medicare three days before I got hitched, which sounds like something an old person might do, which does not describe adorably ageless me. I mostly love being in the third third of my life, as it is the easiest that life has ever been, except for, well, the bodily aspects, and the dither and fogginess, and I wouldn't go back a year—well, maybe back one year, before the two UN reports, which have changed everything.

At our wedding were all the people we love most in the world, gathered in a redwood grove to celebrate the miracle that Neal and I had found each other—needles in haystacks; wrinkly, mulish needles—and fallen in love, and toughed out some conflicts. We celebrated and overate, while outside the sacred circle our nation and the world seemed to have reached the point of no return.

So we danced.

That was glorious and I hate to be a downer but now what? Where on earth do we start to get our world and joy and hope and our faith in life itself back? Where can we again find belief in redemption and confidence that our new grandchildren will have breathable air and dry land on which to thrive and raise their own families? Will our great-grandchildren need gas masks? And is anyone in charge here anymore? If so, we'd like to know how to rise up, how to help restore all that the locusts have stolen—the earth, the oceans, democracy—even with our sore feet, hearing loss, stiff fingers, poor digestion, stunned minds, broken hearts. We are ill with shock and awe. I am

frequently reminded of García Márquez's master-
piece *Love in the Time of Cholera* and of Yeats's
cry in 1919 that the center cannot hold. Yes, these
are times of great illness and distress. Yet the center may just hold.

I can simply tell you where my own rising up
began. It was at the San Diego airport, not that
long ago.

I had left my house fairly early that morning
for the San Francisco airport, feeling distant from
my nice new husband, although I'm not sure he
was aware of this, which is doubly annoying. We
had had a stressful talk a few nights before, and
let's say it had not been beautifully resolved. He
stubbornly resisted my thoughts on some adjust-
ments he might make to his life. The gall! In my
defense, I had had these same thoughts for the
two and a half years we had been together, but
now we were married. We were stuck with each
other. At such a time, a girl's thoughts naturally
turn to annulment, but we are not Catholic and
are thus deprived of this option.

The morning sky was pearly, with a broad ribbon of white below, so you thought it was going to
be cold, but it was warm. You knew the sun was in
there somewhere, inside all that murk that was

going on, and every so often it pecked a hole from inside the eggshell and appeared.

All the way from the airport in San Diego to my hotel, and all the way to a huge white tent holding a thousand women, I waited for my husband to text the exact right words, although I was not sure what those would be. "Darling, you are the world to me, and I'm chagrined that I have resisted your excellent suggestions on how I might best live; from now on I will do whatever I can to accommodate your tiny control issues and alleviate your extreme anxiety and self-loathing."

All the women under the tent were pleasant and intelligent people, some of whom had been paid to assist my befuddled self into the room, get me mic'd and onto the stage, and the rest of whom had paid to hear what I had to say. And almost to a person they followed their greeting with "How's married life?"

This is absolutely all I have heard since I got married. What is the correct answer, especially when you have been living together for almost two years and are not, at the moment, convinced it was a necessary change, as the new husband is a know-it-all and does not obey your will, and

sneezes too loudly, like a howler monkey with allergies?

"Great," I kept answering, to make the question-
ers happy. But what is it really like, one month in?
Is it supposed to be this ordinary, where you're
still mostly madly in love, and you've never met
someone so brilliant who is also kind ninety-five
percent of the time, but who is as set in his annoying ways as you are in yours? We got married with
the Trump blimp flying figuratively overhead,
plus there's always laundry, where your husband
throws your delicate sweater in the wash in a
brutish and male way, or you leave a pen in your
pants pocket and Dalmatian the whole load, and
the dog may have gotten old and sick while you
weren't looking.

Sitting onstage next to the very lovely woman
who was going to interview me, I asked in a whisper what the first question was going to be, and
she enthused, "How's married life?"

I loved the faces of the women under the tent,
the whole gamut in age, looks, fashion, and I
wanted to tell them the exact thing. I am always
hoping that at church or in spiritual meetings
someone will say the exact right thing that will

save me from my bad mind and worries that day. I ask myself what that might be. A pastor friend once told me of her grandfather, who had been a minister, too. When she was young, a friend asked her what he did. She replied, "Every Sunday he stands in front of everyone and tells them that they are beautiful, and God loves them exactly the way they are, and they really don't have to worry, because they all have each other. But then by Tuesday they forget this, so on Sunday he goes back to their church and tells them that they are beautiful, and God loves them just the way they are, and they don't have to worry because they all have each other."

This is what I told the women in the tent, the women in pearls, Doc Martens, Chanel, buzz cuts. Many of them had bright streaks and stripes of magenta, aqua, green in their hair, even the otherwise conventional and elderly. It was a garden. I told them my stories of mess and redemption, because stories can be our most reliable medicine. I told them that, yes, it was going to be really hard to turn the environment around, but that we can do hard and in fact we have done hard before—World War II, vaccines, antibiotics, antiretrovirals. We are up to this.

PROLOGUE: RIBBONS

They asked what the new husband was like, and I described him. He protects and excites and sees me. He takes care of me. He makes me laugh. He and I share the belief that beyond the visible world is a truer realm, one that calls to us both. And we also split the chores. They asked what will save us all, what will turn the barge around from the current ugliness toward a better destination: good old decency and kindness. I could tell that the women felt scared and sad, about America but also their own lives. They worried that they had squandered their lives, and they grieved at how quickly the years had flown by.

I did not know the exact right thing then, but at sixty-six I continue to believe that love is sovereign here, and that the hardest work we do is self-love and forgiveness. I know to serve the poor, to reach for beauty, and to rest. I know salvation will be local, grassroots, and it will be magnified as more people wonder whether maybe they can help.

Sometimes the poor are in pearls, I said. Look around and see whom you can serve. This will fill you. Never give up on intimate friendships or science or nature. They have always saved us, and they will again. And love is the mastermind of it all: "The soul of genius," Mozart reputedly said, "is love, love, love." We need to stop racing and to savor beauty, to look up from our screens at the weather, one another's faces, the ocean, the desert, a garden, and architecture, which is another kind of garden.

The women seemed to love my pitch and bought lots of books (Jesus's last words having been, "Always be selling"). I signed books and gave hugs and smiled in selfies, and managed not to turn my phone on afterward, at least not while anyone was watching.

I was really happy at the end of my talk because I was going straight to the airport for an early-evening flight and would land at eight thirty and be home with my perfectly imperfect husband by ten p.m. I would wake up the next morning in our gigantic bed with a sleeping kitten mashed against my hip. The weather would have winked, changed from the low fuzzed-up gloom I had left in, as if to say, "See, I'm not so serious after all!" Whoever plays with the broad brush might have created a swatch of blue.

I got dropped off at the airport in a better mood than I had arrived in. In the third third of life, you may become just as miserable and prickly as ever, but you cycle through more quickly. You remember other dark nights of the soul and how by dawn they always broke. You discover that everything helps you learn who you are, and that this is why we are here. You roll your eyes at yourself more gently. You sigh and go make yourself a cup of tea.

I was fine when the plane was first delayed, by only forty-five minutes. Maturity is retaining a modicum of grace when you do not get your own way. Also, maturity is hope. I hoped to be in bed by eleven. I texted my husband to let him know. He responded with a sad emoji face. I don't really like, or ever use, emojis, but marriage is one compromise after another and I let it go.

I wandered benevolently around the airport, enveloped in the cloud of smells: french fries and cigarette butts, sugarcane fields on fire and aftershave, anxiety and weariness and patience, and cheap meat on grills. I know the secret of life: If you want to have loving feelings, do loving things. So I flirted with one and all, joshing and complimenting. I was pleased by myself. I got too happy. I decided to make lemonade with the extra forty-five minutes and have my toenails done.

I had gotten a pedicure for the wedding, of

course, just over one month before, and the polish had held up through the honeymoon in Hawaii. But recently I significantly chipped my right big toenail, which was also definitely too long now, so I looked like a three-toed sloth bridesmaid. I googled the airport nail salon, which was nearby and open for another hour and a half. Perfect!

The middle-aged woman in an ersatz nurse uniform at the salon was just finishing a manicure as I bounded up to her. I asked happily if I could be next, even though it was obvious that I would be.

"Oh, sorry, I'm going to close up early tonight."

I drew my head back, like a dowager. "Excuse me?" I asked, as if she had suggested we mate.

"I'm sorry," she said, and turned back to her customer.

"I don't think you're allowed to do that," I said. "The hours are posted right here."

She looked up to find me pointing to the "Hours" sign on the wall, like Goody Proctor or Perry Mason. The other customer started blowing on her nails like they were birthday candles. Time stopped. I said in my most awful voice, the inside mean voice with which I judge myself or tell myself I'll never write again, "How can you do that?"

I will go to my grave thanking Jesus that my son was not there to witness this. The blood would have drained from his face.

The woman just smiled sweetly at me with suppressed hostility and kept working with the other customer.

I slunk away in victimized self-righteousness.

Right then came the text from the airline about the second delay.

My plane would not board for two more hours.

My heart sank and I growled. The only appropriate response was to buy a one-pound bag of York peppermint patties. So I did, and sat down in one of those patented comfortless airport chairs and ate about a dozen, until my throat grew minty fur.

Then I walked to the gate to verify the flight delay for myself. When I got there, I saw a family of three sitting down: an Asian man of forty or so, who may have had a stroke, as his hand was gnarled and his arm was drawn up close against his chest, beside a blonde wife and a child with fair skin and black hair. We made small talk about the hopelessness of air travel while the girl, who was maybe ten, looped a hair ribbon around her neck and appeared to hang herself. Her mother good-naturedly slapped at her hand, making her drop the noose.

I left them and alternately walked around the airport and sat reading, gloomy and aggrieved.

When we finally boarded two hours later, the girl had the hair ribbon tied into a cat's cradle, bridging her hands. And when we were all bustled off the plane an hour and a half later, still in San Diego, she had the ribbon tied between her armpit and her shoulder like the braided cord attached to an epaulet. Her eyes were barely open.

The gate agent told us our flight would leave in the morning and—good news—we could use the same boarding passes we already had. How great.

I got a room at an airport hotel near the harbor, not knowing how I'd get through the night. I texted my husband again. He was so dear and sympathetic that I sort of liked him again.

Once, newly sober, thirty-three years earlier, at an airport hotel in Miami, where I had given a talk at some book association convention, I found myself alone at midnight, twenty stories up, thinking about drinking everything in the minibar and then jumping off the balcony. But something—life? grace?—had one other idea: to pick up the hotel phone and let someone enter into the mess of me. There was an all-night hotline for addicts and alcoholics, so I called that. A young man answered, listened, and said he would send a sober woman to my hotel. It sounded like a nightmare to me, and also unlikely: a stranger was going to come to my room at midnight?

And by God, an elderly woman with a frosted bouffant and a strong Texas accent arrived at my door half an hour later. We got to know each other a little, and then she asked if there was anything I needed to get off my chest. I hadn't thought so, but I spent the next hour telling her terrible things I had done drunk, and terrible things I thought sober (and still do). She nodded a lot and then told me her version of the same scary behavior common to female alcoholics. I felt saved. Before she left, she fluffed up my pillows, turned down my bedspread and blanket, and put a glass of water next to my bed. She must have been forty years older than I, with twenty-five years' sobriety. I told her, "I can't ever repay your kindness," and she said, "Can't never could." At two that morning I walked her out to her car, which turned out to be a pink Cadillac convertible.

I had seen the face of God (and also Her car), in Her distressing guise as a Texan.

The Texan came to me again that night in San Diego. What would she do? Get her guest a toothbrush and toothpaste at the front desk. Fluff up the pillows, turn down the bed, put a glass of water on the nightstand.

First thing in the morning, I tried to call my husband, but he didn't pick up. Then I got a text that our flight had been delayed twenty minutes. I hung my head. At our gate, the Asian father sat sleeping in his seat while his sleepy-looking wife and child chatted. Some of the other passengers from the night before waved. We were a community now—a tired, grumpy community. I fit right in with the poor huddled masses at Gate 17: Not fair! I thought being newly married meant you were exuberant most of the time, even if things went bad. "Are you happy now?" Carrie Fisher was once asked, when she had been clean and sober awhile. She replied, "Happy is one of the things I am most days." But I hadn't been happy much for several days, least of all today.

What would the woman from Texas, God in Her pink Cadillac, recommend? Do kind things for myself in her stead. Tell someone I trusted what was going on. Let someone in. Ugh. Clean my own side of the street.

So I got a yogurt parfait, powdered my nose and put on some lipstick, texted a close friend to ask if she had a minute.

"Of course, honey. Hey! How's married life?"

I had to close my eyes and do my Lamaze.

I texted back, "My flight was delayed 14 hours. I'm exhausted. Neal and I had a rough patch right before I left, now I can't reach him, and I know he's dead or with another woman. I think I have buyer's remorse."

"Ah!" she exclaimed. "Right on schedule. I was wondering when this would kick in."

I was taken aback. This had not occurred to me, my extreme exotic ordinariness.

After a minute, she texted, "Tell me why you're harshing him. What stories are you telling yourself about him?"

I thought this was very rude, what with me in my current tragic condition. I started to resent her, too. Then I realized the common denominator was me. So I did what the Texas lady said to do:

I blurted out my grievances—all the secret ways I judge him, all the ways I judge me for judging him. Also, that he acts very superior sometimes for such a spiritually evolved man. Also, while we were at it, that he locks the bathroom door when he does his morning toilette; I listen to his electric toothbrush and shaver, and the shower, wondering why he would lock out his perfectly nice new wife? Maybe he was shooting heroin in there. And this guy thing, not specific to him, but he never wipes his glasses when they are all smudged. How can he see through the lenses when they're like a motorcycle windscreen after a ride through the desert? He doesn't wear sunscreen and likes to get a tan, even though my father died of melanoma, so it is very triggering for me. Also, when we have an argument and I am explaining my position, he tilts his head in a domineering male way, and if you read between the lines, you can tell he's thinking that you can't possibly think that, because it's so stupid that if you actually thought it, people would have to kill you. Also, he puts butter on absolutely everything, although it is fattening. He cooks white rice with butter, and then serves it with butter.

"That must be a nightmare for you," my friend

texted. "Especially the smudged glasses. And the butter!"

"Relationships are hard."

"I know. But I think you've forgotten that he's your friend."

Wait, *what?*

This stopped me in my tracks. I believe my mouth dropped open.

"Could you say that again?"

"He's your friend," she texted back. "He's your friend that you get to sleep with and wake up with. That's what married life is at its most basic. A friend, your teammate, a person you trust and look forward to talking to, about anything. Someone who seems to really, really like you, who you like, too."

Like? What an odd idea. That's not what I wanted. I thought it was supposed to be more *Barefoot in the Park*, less lifey. I don't want life to be about finding out who I am. That doesn't work for me at all. I want my life to be about doing well and feeling mildly euphoric a lot of the time, and being a do-gooder, loved and admired by everyone. Also, if I was being honest, I'd like to get my weight down, and for my dog not to have gotten so old, and for God to give me answers and freedom, instead of just some old trusted friend to tell my terrible secrets to.

"You're going to feel better now," she continued. Even though she couldn't see me, I shook my head at how much I think I know and how little I actually do know.

The day before, when I'd left for the San Francisco airport, I thought I'd been driving toward a filmy marine layer from the coast, but later I could tell that there were individual clouds, dangling like parts of a mobile against the black hills. It wasn't fog at all. And I'd thought the Asian man was so unfortunate to have had a stroke so young, while right then his daughter wrapped his inert arm in her all-purpose hair ribbon, roping it like a calf and finally making him smile.

So to answer my earlier question of where on earth we begin to recover our faith in life, in the midst of so much bad news and dread, when our children's futures are so uncertain: We start in the here and now. That's why they call it the present. We start where our butts and feet and minds are. We start in these times of incomprehensible scientific predictions, madness and disbelief, aging and constantly nightmarish airport delays, and we look up and around for brighter ribbons.

One

✦

SOUL
LATHER

✦

I got sober in the darkest summer of my life, more than half my lifetime ago. I woke up sick on an already hot morning in my minuscule houseboat in Sausalito with gulls and pelicans taking off and landing outside my window and a clear view of Angel Island. I wanted to die. My best idea was a cool refreshing beer, to get all the flies going in one direction, as my late friend Jack once put it. I do not know what possessed me to call him that day, but I did, and he came over, we talked for a few hours about our alcoholism, and somehow I haven't had a drink since.

My body felt better after a week of sobriety, but it took a long time for my soul to be restored. First I needed to learn to pay bills, take care of my teeth, dispose of a shoe box filled with sedatives

and speed, clean up the moral and financial wreckage of my past.

Defeat has been, for so many of us, the portal
to soul.

I have a friend whose daughter accidentally
killed a man a few years ago, and then tried to
run. Ali was driving home drunk on New Year's
Eve and hit a pedestrian in a crosswalk. I could
have easily run over someone, too. I ran over a dog
or a cat one night forty years ago, on the way to
the only bar in the hippie town where I lived, but
I did not have the courage to stop the car. Maybe it
was a raccoon. At any rate, I drove on, electrified
with fear and guilt. I was twenty-four at the time,
almost ten years younger than Ali when she killed
the man. My dad was dying of brain cancer in our
tiny cabin up on the Mesa, I had just sold my first
book, and in terror, I couldn't do any better than
to speed on. Ali sped on, but a witness got her li-
cense plate.

I had been on the same road a few times already earlier that day forty years ago, to teach a
tennis lesson and clean a house. The road was
curvy, above the beach, lined with eucalyptus
and nasturtiums, a constant interplay of light and
shade, and teasing glimpses of the ocean. There

was a monarch butterfly grove there, veils of black, orange, and white clutching the trunks of trees, at rest or clustered together for warmth, fluttering, undulating. In the past few years, drought and climate shifts have caused them to stop landing there during their migration.

Ali lived near a famous monarch grove, too, in Huntington Beach, with her mom. Everyone liked her a lot, but she was always finding fault with her own creative efforts, her studies, her body, and she had become directionless since dropping out of college. She hung out with her friends, smoked dope, worked odd jobs, went to outdoor concerts.

She was caught, convicted, and sentenced to two years in a prison two hours' drive from her mother's cottage in Riverside. It wasn't Robben Island, but it was hideous enough, all concrete blocks and isolation. A short, slight woman in her thirties, with dimples, Ali was nearly catatonic when she entered prison, except when she was in sheer terror.

I told my kids at Sunday school about her because the prison restored her soul.

"You've all had incredibly sad things happen," I said. "You've all had disappointments. Maybe you've shut down a little, or had to pretend you were just fine all the time. This can make our souls feel cloudy, like a streaky crystal ball."

A hand shot up. I smiled. When you've been teaching Sunday school for as long as I have, you know when you've hit upon a great topic.

"What is our snack today?"

Oh, well. Cherries and chips. Three thumbs up.

The kids in my class have had significant challenges: a crazy mother, absent fathers, a disabled brother, depression. Some of the older teenage girls who have passed through our Sunday school have already been through rehab, and some have been cutters. And when there aren't actual hardships in a child's life, it's still just damaging here on earth. Someday they will also feel smudged by the detritus of addictions, regrets, obsession with finances, chronic guilt about having failed their grown kids, sorrow over the state of their current marriage or guilt about earlier ones. Even now, they know that the world leaves grubby fingerprints all over everything: our hearts, minds, hope.

What would soul Windex look like? This is what I wanted to talk to the kids about. Who are we, and why aren't we being that person? How would we know? When I was a kid, the grown-ups in charge conveyed that we were our manners, what we succeeded at, failed at, looked like, how we obeyed, how we measured up.

What was so threatening for our parents that they avoided mentioning soul? The concept may have been too woo-woo and esoteric, and unstructured. And they couldn't control it or grade it. It was spacy and daydreamy. I was, too, and I was chastised for that. We got hijacked into socialization. Maturing meant conforming to a million rules set by our parents, away from a more seamless participation in life. We had to be herded back to the road from the hedgerows, where, if we were not careful, we would still be living out our days, mostly trying to avoid driving into ditches or being late for important appointments. Ali and I shared a struggle with perfectionism, the most toxic condition for the soul. The next most toxic is the ensuing and chronic contempt for oneself, the belief that one is secretly defective and less-than. The next is the obsession that one is right and better-than.

I told the kids about Ali, what an ordinary person she had been, and then what she had done. The girls put their hands over their mouths.

"Do you think she can ever forgive herself?" I asked.

They agreed, oh, no, absolutely not, not only for killing the man, but also for running.

"Well, would you forgive her?"

They looked at one another.

"It's okay if you wouldn't, especially if you knew the guy she killed. So how could she possibly begin to forgive herself?"

Pause.

"I'll tell you," I continued. "She made a friend."

These kids' friends are their entire lives. All they want is to be with them, or on the phone, talking or texting. They don't particularly want to be with their parents anymore; horribly, they don't even want to be with their grandmothers as much. Yet hanging out with their buddies downtown instills them with friendly watchfulness and curiosity, the very qualities of soul.

All those years ago I'd made a mess of my life, although unlike Ali's, the outside package was successful, and even inspiring, with beautiful views. I betrayed my core values, and women friends who stayed at home with their kids while I partied with their husbands. I thought that I was beyond redemption, but I became friends with a few wild sober women, who insisted that my mind was not always to be trusted: half the time it was for entertainment purposes only. My mind was not who I was. I thought I was nuts and pathetic. The sober women said we all were. They said my soul was fine inside the rubble. They would help me clear it away, and when my cup had begun to fill again, I would pay it forward.

The soul is the lighthouse from which we see the vast celestial ocean, a kiosk from which we observe whatever passes by, the purest expression of our being alive, the one part they couldn't wreck, in the paranoid sense of the word "they." Charles Bukowski said, "If you don't have much soul left and you know it, you've still got soul." Plato said a soul is immortal and imperishable. My new husband—who still reads Plato, if you can believe it—is prone to the random Obi-Wan pronouncement, and he says that the soul is made of friendly awareness and the awareness of that awareness.

One of my Sunday school kids, a twelve-year-old, recently said she sees the soul as being like Pikachu, "a cat-bunny creature, kind and curious." The other twelve-year-old saw it as Casper the friendly ghost. A fifteen-year-old boy with acne said it's a tiny golden snow globe. I wrote all these down, for myself as well as for my own belief that the soul is a location, T. S. Eliot's still point, with a lorgnette.

Is the soul damaged by acne, political madness, rigid or unloving parents? I think so, damaged but not mortally so. It becomes callused, barricaded, yet it's always there for the asking, always ready for hope. Some poet once wrote that we think we are drops in the ocean, but that we are really the ocean in drops, both minute and everything there is.

Certain qualities are of soul, and not mind or culture. Curiosity is one way we know that our souls are functioning. So is a deep goodness. So is presence. When the soul is functioning properly, it tugs on your pant leg to slow down, but otherwise it observes, mostly quietly, but sometimes with its mouth hanging open and a wiggly fascination and sometimes with outright bliss.

I met my beloved two months before the election of 2016, so these years since have been a mixed grill: peaceful and joyous, romantic, crazy and hard. Marriage has helped me feel safe, in having been found by a kind man whom I love to talk with, my soul free to relax into the ploppy comfort of being known—of someone being so *on* to me, except when I am fixated on the fate of the earth or Neal's suspicious mole and imminent death.

I have several soul-mate friends, but living with my best friend gave my soul permission to surface in a new if sometimes tentative way. It has made me softer, less armored, way less of a perfectionist, since Neal sees me in my natural state almost all the time, slothful, gluttonous bear that I am. I can't even pretend to be my impressive public self. No wonder some of our parents forgot to mention soul, as it is apt to distract one from Serious Goals and Aspirations. It is as playful and illogical as a kitten, as watchful as God or a baby. It rubs its back lazily against trees. It stops and gasps at beauty and is bathed in it. And sometimes it begins to weep.

The soul is the thing underneath that is so hard to express, because it is so far from regular expressable human endeavors. Rumi comes consistently closest. The teacher Adyashanti said that the part of you that sees that you are afraid *isn't* afraid. It's that watchful part in our consciousness that knows, that remembers to look up from the bar and the computer desk, the schedules and the phone.

I had one of the Sunday school girls read Mark

8:36, "What does it profit a man to gain the whole world, but lose his soul?" Jesus says the soul is more important than the entire world. It is essence, pure love, our candle, our participation in the illimitable, our goodness.

One of the kids said the soul is no color and every color; another kid said it was clear. I have felt my soul go gray. The drinking and eating disorders, the deadening relationships I couldn't escape, the regrets about my parenting. My closest friends all have guilt and pain about their grown children, and financial anxiety, and existential sorrow at how quickly it all goes, how in a blink the children have grown and can still be mean to them—to adorable martyred them—after all they've done for them!

My Sunday school kids love how quickly life goes. They can't wait to be older and older. They love things to go faster—my story, for example. They're getting bored now. They want a chase scene, but as they also want their snack, they will hang in with me a while longer.

Marcus Aurelius said that we are little souls carrying around corpses. This is my understanding, but it's too scary for these kids, and besides, no one looks less corpsey than the kids in the class. I might ask them about places they've been where beauty has made them catch their breath. A mountaintop? The ocean? The redwoods? Where inside them does awe arise? Soul is a place, the innermost Russian nesting doll.

I promised that after our snack we'd go outside and have soul time. Deal? I asked. They sighed: Deal.

So, I continued, Ali made a friend, a lifer in the same cell block, who happened to have gotten sober in prison. The friend was tall and strong and kept an eye out for her, shared books with her, and took her to meetings of Alcoholics Anonymous. Ali explained to the other women in the first few meetings that she was not actually an alcoholic, just a social drinker with bad luck. I love this in a person. I was just the same. The other prisoners nodded politely.

On one visit from her mother, when she shared with her this belief and her attendance at meetings, the mom said the most amazing thing a mother can say. She held back her scared, controlling opinions and denial with her. She nodded politely and said, "Huh."

Ali kept going to meetings with her friend, because it got her out of the cell for an hour a few times a week, and the women at the meetings laughed and hugged. She was still depressed, flattened by what she had done, how it had damaged her victim's family and her own; by the year left to serve and the dismal future.

How could life possibly degrease Ali's soul? The same way it has always degreased mine, although our circumstances are so different. Yeats wrote that soul might louder sing "for every tatter in its mortal dress." You want mortal dress? Try prison garb.

But on the day Ali said she might just possibly be an alcoholic, when she said who she was, or might actually be, something flared: the pilot light, a watch fire. Ali still smelled the terrible smells, heard the clang and cacophony of captivity, but a switch had gone on. She looked up, away from the grime of her floor and plastic prison slippers, to the window.

Her blood alcohol level had not been that high at the time of the accident, .12, definitely above the legal limit but probably not drunk-drunk. I drove hundreds of times with higher levels than that; all of us bon vivants did at the time. I never got a DUI. I did get two fix-it tickets while in blackouts, as I discovered the next day. In our childhoods, the local police drove our drunk fathers home, handed them over to us at the front door if our mothers were asleep. But Ali was born in a time when we throw the book at drunk drivers, especially those who kill or maim, and that's a good thing. Ali's sentence almost seems extreme, given who she is, but she *killed* a man and left the scene of the crime.

What did the Sunday school children think should have happened to Ali? One boy said that while Jesus would have forgiven her—the boy's tone suggesting Jesus was kind of a wuss that way—he himself would not be able to, because of the cowardice. The girls tended to feel sorry for everyone, as do I: the victim, his family and friends, Ali.

Oh, the cowardice stories I could tell! How much of me I've kept hidden, out of fear of rejection; how warily I've let out my kite string; how often I hold my breath in fear. Wedge me open, I pray.

These kids will have their own cowardice stories someday. We all do. The fear of dying, of living, of making mistakes, of being known, of anyone anywhere being mad at us. I'm so brave in many ways that it can make people teary, and so often afraid.

The odds are that the kids will not screw up at the same level Ali did, destroying the happiness of an innocent victim's family, and burning her own family's social and financial lives to the ground. But it goes without saying that they will make some bad decisions and big mistakes, which will hurt people they love. Our social system says there are certain actions you cannot be forgiven for, and for which you must feel self-loathing the rest of your life. But, I told the boy in class, the justice system is quid pro quo, and after a year of legal wrangling, Ali was sentenced to two years in prison, and after that, she will have paid her debt. Who are we to judge, as Pope Francis keeps reminding us. A lot of people might wonder how she could not be required to hate herself, and they get to wonder that.

The nearly impossible work that Ali faces— and that we all face—will be to forgive herself. This will take time. Time takes time. I hate this.

One of the girls had an idea: Ali could devote the rest of her life to helping people. Wow, I said. Yes. That is exactly what redemption looks like:

love in service. So how, besides service to those who are afraid or suffering, do we connect with this place inside us, this infinitesimal speck of the celestial?

The kids looked at one another, puzzled. How can we feel it when we're down or flattened by hard times or stuck in enervated lives? Where do we start?

What about noticing when your mother holds you for no reason, I said, and you curl into her? Both twelve-year-olds nodded, the fifteen-year-old not so much. What about when you feel awe, under the stars, or on a mountaintop, or at the Grand Canyon, or on the beach outside San Quentin? Have you seen a monarch butterfly grove, thousands of stained-glass-window wings? Yes, they nodded. They knew what it meant to be blown away.

What does it feel like when you roll down a hillside and the dizziness goes away, and you're lying there in the grass looking up at the hill and the sky?

One of the kids yawned. I sensed that time was running out for me.

"Okay, two more things. Don't you feel a version of that when you sit with your back against a tree?" They nodded. "Well, who is feeling that? I have a brainstorm: Let's go sit with our backs against trees, together."

"It's time for snacks," the fifteen-year-old protested. He was going to lead an armed insurrection against me. The girls looked as pitiful as basset hounds.

"Let me just tell you how the Ali story ends. Then we'll eat." There is bitterness, and there are more sighs. Sighs are the punctuation of most of our lives, of relief, of how much worse it could have been, of "Now what?"

When Ali had one year sober, she and her friend got to be part of the volunteer conservation work program run by the California Department of Corrections and Rehabilitation. They made a few dollars a week. The kids were contemptuous— the girls make ten dollars an hour *babysitting*. "It doesn't sound like great money," I told the kids, "but you know what it bought her over time? It bought her herself. And a skill. And a purpose: to save other families and wildlife. She couldn't bring back what she had taken from the victim's family or her own, but she could be a helper in the world."

The kids were all but making the universal gesture of "Speed it up."

So I did.

"Not long ago, Ali and a crew of inmates were cleaning up fallen branches and debris after a nearby river overflowed following torrential rains, when guess what she found in some brush." The kids really didn't seem to care. What ev. A snake? Doubloons? "A baby coyote."

They look up—I've surprised them. "She brought it out to show the other workers on the crew, and the chief shouted, 'Look what Ali Baba found! A baby coyote.'"

They smile. It's very cool.

The chief called a wildlife rescue organization, and brought them the baby when work was done for the day. How it is possible to go from being convict D53789 to Ali Baba, from maximum shame and cowardice to protector of baby coyotes and her newborn sober self, both worthy to be saved? Something had to have opened.

One boy put a fistful of tortilla chips on a paper towel in front of each of us, a girl poured paper cups of water, and another girl placed a wooden bowl of cherries in the center of the table where

we can all reach them. They were delicious beyond words. When I got sober all those years ago I
started to taste the world again, the fruits and
salty crunch, fresh air and smoke and everything
in between. Each cherry tastes different because
they ripen at different times, some sweeter, some
tarter, but all dark red and heart-shaped.

I raised my cup and reached out over the
wooden bowl so we could touch paper cups in a
toast: Open, sesame.

Two

+

THE
KITTEN

+

Everything and not much has changed since my husband and I toasted each other at our wedding. The kitten was nine months old at the time, crazy as a baby March hare. On our wedding night she raced back and forth over us like a flying red horse until she passed out. She woke us on our first morning as husband and wife with a furious and extended bout of pouncing practice. When Neal and I started our second trimester, she turned one. We are hopeful that any minute now she will start demonstrating the rich inner life for which cats are famous.

When Neal asked me to marry him, on our two-year anniversary of falling in love, it took me a full minute to answer. To begin with, when he asked me if he could ask a question, I thought it had to do with what kind of patio pebbles we should order. I was still sad and shaken by the loss of our beloved cat a month before, when we had been traveling for too long and he had escaped our cat sitter and had either gone off to join the Merchant Marine or been eaten by coyotes. And I've seen very few good marriages in my life, and though Neal has all the qualities I had only dreamed of, I had grave reservations about getting married.

But he has a depth of kindness that is the answer to all spiritual questions and the appropriate response to all problems. Just ask the Dalai Lama. It's his only religion. He is also brilliant, which is exciting, and he depends on nature as medicine, as do I. And he's good at lounging around, which I love in a guy.

So after gaping at him on our couch for a minute, I replied, "Could we get a cat?" He nodded.

"Okay," I replied, "I'll marry you."

We had already been living together for a year. A wedding would be a chance to celebrate the miracle of having found each other. And a new cat! So yes yes yes. It was just like in the movies, for about half an hour.

We called this plan the Cat Codicil. A few months later, we got a five-month-old tabby kitten, named her Rosalie, and began to raise her as our own. We got her fancy cat toys and dozens of felt mice, but she hid most of them, and instead focused her bloodlust on a long wire twist tie from a sack of Costco tortilla chips. Curly pastel gift-wrap ribbons cause her to lose her mind. She shreds raffia, eats it, throws up.

She got bigger and bigger. Neal and I got married.

Both have been interesting learning experiences, the marriage slightly more so.

I had forgotten how disconcerting intimacy can be, how rare and how devastating the potential for loss that's inherent in it. The old adage is that *intimacy* means "Into me I see"—deeply, with a flashlight—and believe me, we're not trying to avoid seeing the lovely and selfless aspects of ourselves. It's not even the unlikable qualities— narcissism, fraudulence, envy. It's the really disgusting, uncooked-egg parts of us—wanting people to fail, using people, holding on to resentments, our sense of entitlement.

And Neal has all of those uncooked-egg parts, too. We all do. It comes with being human. My pastor calls it our dual citizenship, how we have the human passport with all our biographical details and neuroses engraved on it, and the heavenly one, as children of the divine.

Neal "sees" both passports, my papers. You don't need to be married to let someone see you, as I have let several friends see me, and they have let me see them. But if you are married, you are stuck with the person. They consider "my house" to be "their house." Even if they begin to wear on you, they won't be going "home." Marriage means you *are* their home.

Neal believes that my spiritual identity is the truth of who I am, ageless and childlike, but he also observes my gravest personality defects with forbearance. We both practice the acronym WAIT, as in "Why am I talking?"—although I weaponize my silences while he grows thoughtful. And then there is my dear old aging body, sagging and bag-ging, plus the terrible damage of my having grown up on tennis courts in the hot California sun. My crepey arms are the price I pay for having been a tennis star. He doesn't see that. Instead, he sees the arms of his wife, arms that hold him in a way he has never been held before. I worriedly hold them up to within two inches of his nose and de-mand that he notice and, ideally, recoil.

He says, "Some of us got more sun than others growing up."

What kind of crazy, aggressive shit is that?

When I am watching him, I observe what a tall, nice-looking, thoughtful, focused know-it-all he is. He comes from a family of know-it-alls. His brothers are just like him. I love them, but at our family vacations it is like Wikipedia with PMS.

When I am *seeing* him, I intuit something deep inside him, wounded and perfect. Seeing is a form of pure being, unlike watching or looking at. Seeing is why we're here.

I first observed his know-it-all-itis within two weeks of our falling in love, and when I called him on it, he teared up. It was an aspect of his character that had always eventually come up, ruinously, in his past intimate relationships. (Not that he had ever had any others before me.) On this revelatory Sunday, he had agreed to come to church with me. He stayed in the service while I took a few kids off to the children's church room. When we met in the courtyard later, he got on to the subject of Mother Mary's Immaculate Conception. I had always believed it meant Jesus's virgin birth. But it doesn't, and in the most know-it-all way, he told me that it means that Mary was conceived without the stain of original sin, because of the graces that flow from Christ.

I was enraged.

He was not even raised Catholic. He just knows a lot about a lot of subjects—all music, all world religions, politics, and science. I'm sure it drives Jesus crazy, too.

I called my Jesuit friend Tom, who confirmed that Neal was right, and that lucky for me, Catholics are allowed to share this insider information with their flinty Protestant friends every few years. The Immaculate Conception has nothing to do with Jesus as a zygote. Mary was not damaged by original sin, unlike other people Tom could think of, and Protestants are capable of understanding this teaching if and only if they ask God for help.

I hate to be wrong, and I hate that I am wrong so often in so many ways, that my thinking is often defensive, judgmental, and skittish. (I have a thinking disorder. I once took a 20 Questions quiz about drinking but substituted thinking and I got most of them: Do you prefer to think alone? Do you hide your thinking from loved ones? Has thinking begun to impact your health and quality of life?) Anyway, I did what one does: I pretended his correcting me was no big deal, while withholding my affection and plotting my revenge.

Yet this was nothing compared with the ugliness of his ensuing correction over what kind of flowers the famed Lilies of the Field were.

I had always thought they were regular old lilies—calla lilies, the kind sold at Easter, the kind you see painted on mugs and pencil cases in Catholic gift shops. We were driving along one day when for no particular reason the great anti-anxiety passage in Matthew came up:

"Consider the lilies of the field, how they grow; they toil not, neither do they spin: And yet I say unto you, that even Solomon in all his glory was not arrayed like one of these."

Neal said, "Jesus did not mean lilies, like the kind we think of. Lilies don't grow in fields. They grow in marshes, grasslands, mountains. Most experts agree the flowers were probably crown anemones."

I studied him behind the wheel for a moment when he announced this. Finally I said, "*Really*, Neal?"

He started to elaborate in his blithely professorial way, but I cut him off and stared grimly out the window, at the passing golden undulating and lilyless fields.

When we got home I looked it up, and of course, horribly, he was right. The flowers to which Jesus referred were probably crown anemones, bright garish poppies, beautiful in a somewhat clownish way.

Calla lilies, on the other hand, are so Jesusy— elegant, tall, and lean, like the older sister all the teachers loved and wished you were more like, with good posture and skin as creamy as the moon.

Neal planted lilies in the great garden he created when we moved into our house before we got married. I had never been married and he had never had a garden: we were virgins. The large yard had somehow managed to be both barren and overgrown at the same time, and Neal painstakingly transformed it into wild beauty, with lots of roses, daisies, gladiolas, and lilies.

The lilies outside our window remind me of chalices, ceremonial containers that you want to hold with both hands so you don't spill the contents, whether it is grog, communion wine, or the fresh garden air. A spiral grows from deep inside in an arabesque way, ending in a wing or hook. A hook, for catching or suspending, and a wing to fly. Lilies are modest, with a teasing restraint, which is how I would describe myself romantically. And wonderfully, they have a phallic yellow stamen, which looks like a Lego piece jammed into all that elegance.

Neal is more an anemone—an unashamed flower, wide open and available. He lives, for the most part, in what is. I live in fear of bad outcomes—of climate catastrophe, war, aneurysms; and of course, snake attack. He tries to reassure me. "There are *no* cobras in Marin. And we can survive the apocalypse, if it lasts less than two weeks."

The center of the crown anemone is outlined in white, like a target. It's sort of a landing strip for the bees. It says, and Neal says, in not so many words, "Come unto me."

He has filled our yard with color and beauty. Also, a peach tree, planted one month before our wedding, on our hill, now bursting with peachy rose-coral fruit, the sweetest, juiciest ever. Where once there was dry rocky dirt, there's now a tree as Asian and gorgeous as a persimmon tree in fall. The squirrels got some of the peaches but my grandson and I got most of them. He doesn't mind when the juice runs down his chin; he wipes it on his strong brown arms and reaches for another.

So if Neal can grow a thriving fruit tree, a tree of beauty that feeds us, I can grow in this marriage. But growing bigger hurts your joints. Growing up is hard.

I didn't even want the kitten to grow up. I liked the peekaboo Christmas-stocking phase. She was Neal's first kitten. He is violently allergic to cats—thus the need for the Cat Codicil. When his hairy ex-girlfriends owned them, he lived with cats by adding brewer's yeast to their food every day. Brewer's yeast changes something mysterious about cats' dander or saliva, and his allergy was reduced significantly. In fact, when we first corresponded at Match.com and I read that he was allergic to cats, I tried to give him the brush-off. He wrote back about his brewer's yeast remedy. I thought he was just trying to get into my pants or had a manuscript he needed help with. But I agreed to have one coffee date and then we almost immediately needed to be together every day. He was at my house all the time, with my huge, affectionate gray-and-white cat, Gringo, whom we dosed, and Neal was able to tolerate him, and then he fell for his cunning feline wiles, and the ballast of holding him.

Rosalie instantly had him wrapped around her finger. I am her Person, but Neal is her Guy. She dances on his chest like a tiny Lipizzaner, spinning, trotting about, trit trot, trit trot, "Want to see my butt, Neal?" Trit trot, trit trot. "Ooh ooh, Neal, you like what you see?" She's baby Charo.

Sometimes she stops the dance and looks over at me. "Oh, hi, Mom."

Then early one morning she was missing.

The kitten has slept with us every night since we got her, and is always asleep against our legs when we first wake. But that morning when I woke, she was gone. Therefore, instantly I believed she was dead. I must have left the front door open at dawn when I let the dog out to pee. She'd been run over, or she'd frozen to death.

Or more likely, been eaten by coyotes.

And it was my fault.

We looked everywhere she had ever hidden, in every closet and even on every shelf that she had been too small to reach before. And we searched the yard.

She was gone. A dark cloud would hang over our wedding, of my having killed Neal's kitten.

Even if we went ahead with the ceremony, there would be an underlying thrum of pain and re-sentment, as in so many marriages I've seen over time. This conviction began to unfold in less than a minute, as soon as I realized that the kitten was not snuggled up against me. It is a familiar feeling for the grown children of alcoholics and the mentally ill, who as young children with in-consistent parents had some small measure of control *only* if they constantly prepared for bad outcomes. Maybe one's parents shouldn't have gone ahead with the second date, let alone the marriage; and they might have been better off raising orchids or teacup poodles instead of kids. But they had us. Commonly, the mothers either caused death by helicoptering, or by caffeinated neglect, and the fathers came home late, desperate to be left alone with a cocktail. At the far extreme, at a birthday party at my friend Pammy's when I was six, her estranged father showed up drunk and smashed her drunk mother, Mary, in the mouth, knocking out a tooth. Pammy grew up with few expectations that things would go a certain way, and so she lived as fully as possible, with the gift of looking at what was right in front of her that might actually nourish her. She did not look to her parents to see her and delight in her. I did, and sometimes still do, look to my parents, although they are long dead. (But why let that stop you?)

Being seen, and seeing who the people in your family were, was ill advised. In fact, the first rule of being the young child of unwell parents was to agree not to see what was going on: in the kitchen, at the dining table, or when the lights went out. My parents did not make loud noises or ever fight, so when they were in bad shape and my brothers and I stood outside their door listening for clues, it was eerie, with unworldly noises and an occasional thump, like at a séance.

Neal and I kept looking for the kitten, inside and out, under every stick of furniture, inside cupboards, over every square inch of the home we've created, every closet, storage space, bookshelf. I prayed and skittered about, while Neal tromped around methodically and said knowing things about kittens and more places to look. A lily and an anemone, under one roof, sharing one fear and one hope.

The kitten was gone, and by the end of an hour-long search, Neal was near tears. He thought she was dead, too. We sat down on the couch, scared and sad but together, which is what intimacy looks like sometimes, in darkness as well as light.

Some days the light is diffuse, and you have to go on faith that more of it is behind the cool gray fog. I don't like this very much.

First I turned on Rosalie: What an idiot, and a raffia-barfing ingrate. And then I turned on a light. Light! I'd forgotten about light. Turn on a light, and not some esoteric inner light. Light light. I turned on the lamps, and waited with hope for our kitten to appear.

But she didn't. She was really gone.

"What else can we do?" I asked Neal, as we huddled like a raggedy old couple in a park. "We can't even post this at Nextdoor.com because we did that when Gringo disappeared for good. Everyone knows he never came back. We can't have lost two cats in two months. People will look at us suspiciously, like, 'There's that death couple one block over.'"

"'You can see fur in their teeth.'" We managed small smiles, the first hint of the movement of grace.

Our family motto is that we never give

up—it's tattooed on my son's forearm—because people didn't give up on us, so Neal and I waited, sad, parched, and each of us secretly much more concerned for the other. I guess that is what love looks like.

Parched! I'd forgotten about water. Light and water, ideally (and biblically) a light rain falling from the skies, or a waterfall, deep calling to deep, or in a pinch, a cool drink from the faucet. Neal brought us each a glass frosted with cold. The ice cubes tinkled, silvery. Light, water, kindness, and not giving up. These are huge; all there is.

And suddenly, like a magic trick, someone was gently nibbling my toes, like those ticklish fish manicures women in Beverly Hills get, but furry. The hilarious, adorable nightmare of a kitten was back; such a funny pansy face. Relief flooded me like a mild hot flash. I had no idea where she could have been hiding, unless there was some wormhole in an alternative universe known only to cats. But she was here, back at work, exploring, tearing up the rug, hiding, exploring, dragging around raffia, pouncing, and then collapsing, sound asleep.

We were as happy as little kids.

"I knew she'd show up again eventually," said Neal, he who knows all things, at least retroactively. But I'll tell you, this little five-pound being had had him going. And being who I am—the same woman to whom he proposed—I will never let him forget this.

Ever since, when one of us is afraid (usually me) of the suffering of someone we love, aging, the terrible heat, the pandemic, or North Korea, the other says, "The kitten isn't dead. The kitten is in the living room." And then the scared one feels okay again briefly, which is all one can really hope for most days. I am going to get a thousand pins made up with these words and hand them out to anxious people like me who feel more sadness and worry than others do. I will save one for you.

Three

᯽

REPENTABILITY

✦

We excel during tragedies, bringing our best selves to serve the suffering in a devastated world, nation, community, family. We keep each other company when children or pets are missing, when our last auntie or old dog dies, while waiting for prognoses. Our human response to each other's hurt and loss is what most gives me hope, along with science and modern medicine. We rise up to help the best we can, and we summon humor to amend ghastly behavior and dismal ongoing reality. Help and humor save us. Goodness and courage are how the divine presents itself so often—whether in drag, as close friends, or as EMTs. They do what Kafka said a book must do: bring an axe to the frozen sea within, or tools to carve an ice-fishing hole.

Hardship is not the problem; we're good at doing hard things.

It's the weirdness of it all that wears me down, the freak shows in Washington, D.C., and Hollywood, the sniper seemingly in the trees picking off friends, my body degenerating over time from athlete to grandma pudding, my lava lamp of a mind.

Just last week, I went back to the nail parlor where I'd gotten a manicure and pedicure for my wedding, a hole-in-the-wall with crosses everywhere. It's not your usual salon with a Buddha altar and waving good-luck Japanese cat. When he saw me, the owner threw his arms around me and asked how the wedding had gone. He remembered! He sat me down at a toenail station and began to run hot water over my feet. We settled in.

While he removed my old polish, I told him about the wedding. He suddenly remembered that my fiancé was not a Christian. Uh-oh. He asked me who the priest had been. I lied. We had had three officiants—a Buddhist, a lapsed Episcopalian, and my irascible Jesuit friend Tom, who told the congregation during the service that I still owed the groom's family twenty goats as dowry. I answered, "Our minister."

He asked, "Wasn't your grandfather a Presbyterian minister?" I nodded, surprised at his memory.

"And wasn't your father an atheist?"

I looked into his face helplessly. It was so *Law & Order.*

"Repentance," he said, "is the word for the day."

Whoa. I hadn't known this. Had he gotten some sort of memo?

But I am not averse. My Sunday school youth group and I have discussed repentance: to change directions so that you don't end up where you are heading, to change your mind in the deepest center of yourself in a way that changes you, so that, as in the Mary Oliver lines, we "never hurry through the world but walk slowly, and bow often."

"You know that your father is in hell now," the man continued matter-of-factly, as he ran a sharp poking device under my big toenail. "Sadly, he did not repent before his death. And it sounds like your new husband is headed there."

My nice new husband! This would be a catastrophe—if I believed there was a hell. We've all been to the one here, in the passages of time marked by terror and sheet-metal loneliness. But I let it pass. What could I say, anyway? "Your wife is a whore. I saw her down the street with Edgar from Sales"? With his sharp poking device now poised above my baby toe?

But I did want to ask, "Hey, do you get many repeat customers?"

Somehow we moved on to other topics, and when I left, my toes were ravishing.

I had my yearly physical a little later. My doctor asked all the usual questions, and checked everything that could be checked, and then had me strip for my melanoma scan. My beautiful father, now barbecuing in hell, died of melanoma that had spread to his brain, so every year my doctor goes over me with a fine-tooth comb. She checked every inch of me, including some very special places. Everything was fine, until she got to my toenails.

"Hmm," she said. "It's too bad you have toe-nail polish on, since melanomas can grow under-neath the nail."

It was critical-mass weirdness. And I began to trip.

To trip is to enter a different state of conscious-ness, where doors of perception open or shift, sometimes, as when you're on drugs and you see the beauty and interrelatedness of all things (or, by the same token, spiders on undulating walls), or in this case, when you see your newly married self as a Day of the Dead bride, a skeleton in a festive wedding dress.

I tried to focus on the rest of my physical but saw lesions growing like mushrooms under my nails.

I've been afraid since birth. I'm not sure I ever bounced back after reading of young Beth's death in *Little Women*. I've been scared of life and my parents' dying for sixty-some years now, and it did not help that this was a day of toenail death. Here my nice new husband was going to hell, and melanomas were sprouting on my nail bed.

So? I did what any sane person would do: got a slab of Safeway carrot cake and numbed out in the car while eating all the frosting off. And when all that sugar kicked in, I smiled.

I was like this as a child, with both the love of sugar and the fearfulness. I was raised to numb out by memorizing or obsessing, and not do airy-fairy things like gaze in wonder or breathe. I was afraid of everything—most men, bad grades, bullies, certain foods. I was even afraid of the carousel at the zoo, which was supposed to delight all children.

Not me. My parents took my brothers and me to Golden Gate Park regularly, and we always had a

ride on the fantastic rare Dentzel carousel. Riding
on it, I often felt helpless, confused, lonely, and in
danger, while faking a good time to make my folks
happy. Round and round, horses with flaring
nostrils, their lips pulled back so they could bite
you, moving up and down so you might fall off.
And the music was unearthly, creepy, though it
was supposed to be jaunty, the way clowns are
supposed to be charming. But both are so scary.

And not to sound petty, but it turned out you
never got the horse you wanted. Someone had
gotten to it first. You got stuck on some loser
horse, or worse, a lion, with its arm-sized mouth
and its golden-red mane you knew would suddenly burst into flames.

I regularly saw my parents waiting by the side
and I longed to be with them, while wishing
they would disappear. They were so embarrass-
ing: grim, or faking happiness when they couldn't
stand each other. I simply was not a good match
for this earth when I was a child. And then when I
was a bit older, I grew so fast that I was in pain and
unstable. When I woke up in the morning, I felt as
though I had to get used to moving in my larger
body. I tripped and ran into walls sometimes.

This has always been true with growing and

changing, even now. It hurts. So my first response is always to resist. I'm not stupid.

I was embarrassed by my parents because my mom was so heavy and both she and my father smoked, yet I needed and wanted them so much while I was on my own very special ride.

No one told me until college that it was an illusion that kids are supposed to be carefree, so I thought I alone was weird, defective, ungrateful. No one told me until college that by the time kids were eleven, when parents hugged them tightly, most kids wished they'd go away, or when their parents left them alone, children wanted them close by. Children felt lonely in their parents' embrace.

After the carrot cake, I got the repentance bug again. Less scaring myself, less cake.

I saw that I am heading (God willing) to a fat old age where I will have spent only twenty percent of any given day paying attention to life, to being where my feet are. The rest of the time will have been spent in the ticker tape of imaginings, a low-level fear about those I love, and the things I need to buy. It is life in Plato's cave, selling other people fancier rocks.

I wanted to repent there and then, in the car with the Safeway bakery box in my lap, as I had when I heard a pastor rewrite the twenty-third psalm as "The Lord is my Shepherd, I shall not trip." I wanted to learn to be.

Then I remembered something a sober diocesan priest named Terry said: "We don't get over much here." So maybe if I couldn't do sackcloth and ashes, I could at least muster ruefulness, rein in my mind to more frequent presence. And I did: You'll often see me with a loose rubber band around my wrist to snap myself back to the present when I am tripping, when I am numbing out on a trance of toxic obsessing.

Minds change all the time. Besides, it's not only toxic and obsessive thoughts that are the problem. Sometimes it's more a foggy slide show about bad people, about foods I crave, the aisles at Target, Neal on life support. When I gently snap my rubber band, it stings my wrist just enough so that I come back to my body, to my soft container.

Booze did this for me as a teenager: it helped me get out of my mind and into my surroundings. My friends and I were at the carousel in Golden Gate Park dozens of times in high school, for rock concerts by Jefferson Airplane, the Grateful Dead, and Quicksilver, and I loved getting on the merry-go-round stoned. But the calliope always bugged me. It sounded like it was coming from a distance, even another realm, all tinny and tarnished, attempting to be cheerful but with an undertone of melancholy, as the time sped by.

I saw another Dentzel carousel later, during college, in Bethesda, Maryland. I was staying with a friend from Goucher College during a three-day weekend, since I couldn't get home, and we were gloriously stoned in Glen Echo Park. The National Park Service had bought the park from the private owners in the 1960s and it was in the midst of renovations, so the carousel wasn't running, but it was a gilded menagerie, a work of art, elaborately carved and painted. The animals were beautiful, their motion frozen as in sculptures. Marvelously carved, tossing their heads, their saddles elaborately decorated. But the eyes scared me, especially because I was stoned and far from home: they were the too-wide eyes of an attacker or a panicked animal. The tiger was ready to chomp on our arms grown fat on dorm food. Even the gigantic rabbits might go rogue and kill you. They could jump off the circular platform and hop down the road with you in their mouths.

Mercifully, we had alcohol in our purses, a pint of Jack Daniel's to share and a beer each.

We had a great wasted joyous day. We chewed Sen-Sen and gum before my friend's mother came to pick us up. It was one of my happiest days ever.

I'm not sure I even heard the name Bethesda again until after I started going to this funny little church in Marin County's poorest town. The preacher preached from time to time on John 5, where Jesus heals the paralytic man who has been ailing for thirty-eight years at the pool of Bethesda, where an angel would swoop down and dip her wing into the waters every day, stirring it up so the first one in would be healed. The pastor said that when the waters of life were stirred up, we could become unblemished.

It was not until a few years later that Father Terry convinced me of the opposite, that we would not get over much here. And that this was not the point—the point was to lean toward goodness, to resist less, to pray for our enemies. The point was to have a spiritual awakening of any sort that helped us live more often in kind awareness. I would rarely be in conformity with the divine's huge crazy love, so I just prayed, Help me start walking in your general direction. And the greatest prayer, Help me not be such an asshole.

If I repented to avoid hell, only my actions

change, not my heart or outlook. If I'm repenting by leaning in closer to life, trying not to focus on everyone and everything that annoy me, then my perspective changes and I'm kinder. I trip out on myself way less often now, and this lets the generosity inside reveal itself. I find a whiff of willingness to grow. Both have come with age, in the third third of my life.

Actually, those sober women, my big sisters, helped me to repent enough, changed me into a saner and more grateful version of myself. Sober people said I didn't have to pick up a drink today and could decide to love a little better, starting with myself. I got repented when I wasn't even looking.

Three years sober, I had a child by myself, with no partner or money, and I had to accept a lot of help with bills, and solidarity with other hilariously imperfect and funny mothers. Paradoxically, those were my favorite years. Eventually my son was too big to sit through regular church, so out of necessity I started a Sunday school. Studying to teach was how I learned to love the story of the paralyzed man at the healing pool in Jerusalem.

There's a man who has been sitting on a mat near the pool, where every day the angel stirs up the water, and the first people get healed. But he never makes it. People rush by and no one gets him to his feet at the water's edge, ready to splash forward. Then Jesus comes by, touches the man who's been waiting for help for thirty-eight years, and says something like "Pick up your moldy, stinky mat and walk, dude . . ." And the man does.

I already believed that prayer could help heal. A number of the old African American ladies from the South in our small congregation who had been diagnosed with terminal diseases lived for years. The bossiest one lived eight years after she was given months to live. I believe in antibiotics and chemo and also in the laying on of hands. So sue me.

But Jesus didn't need water or a magic wand. The man walked right out of the temple area with his mat, and what did he do next?

He ratted out Jesus to the authorities for working on the Sabbath.

The younger Sunday school kids are upset to hear this—it's like the schoolyard. The older kids love it; it's just like them.

No one has ever deconstructed this story for me better than my Jesuit friend Jim Harbaugh.

He said to forget the angel and the waters, that that verse was a later addition to John's Gospel from someone who was hoping to spark a tourist attraction. He said to focus instead on the puzzling behavior of the crippled man.

This is one of John's stories about people who have some faith in Jesus and either grow in faith after their encounter with Him, like the Samaritan woman, or don't, like this guy in John 5, who actually go backward by putting their faith in something worldly and seemingly more powerful than love. Jerusalem at the time was dominated by the priestly aristocracy of the Sadducees, with all the religious and civil power in Israel. (Jesus and his followers are from Galilee in the north, which Father Jim said is more middle- and working-class, and the stronghold of the Pharisees, who are much closer to Jesus—"much less cynical than the Sadducees, who are rich bastards.") The paralyzed man decided to go with the ruling power. I've noticed more than a few people who pick Mitch McConnell over Jesus.

John doesn't tell us why the man can't go beyond his petty small-mindedness (although I often can't either) or why he betrays the only person who ever did him a kindness. That has to remain speculative.

Maybe he didn't have a single friend all those years to help him into the pool. Maybe, as my grandson suggested, he was a just cranky old man and everyone hated him. This is what hell would be like, a whole life without loving friends, maybe a bit like it is for brother Trump. The man had been power-less for a long time, and now he wanted to be affil-iated with people who had power, not some odd homeless guy. The man was obsessed with getting into the water and couldn't adjust to Jesus's way of healing because it wasn't what he had expected all those years. He whined and cast blame, instead of doing what most who approached Jesus said: "Help!"

If you are blind or have leprosy or can't walk, one would think you don't need a cardboard sign to spell out the problem and your desired solu-tion, i.e., to walk. But this would be admitting powerlessness, which was and is the scariest part of getting sober. Finally, if you are lucky, the Gift of Desperation gives you the insight that you're in no position to dicker over how or by whom your sorry ass is going to be saved.

I had to lean away from my own good ideas of salvation and lean toward the people who were staying sober. They said, "Don't drink, and ask God for help." This was miserable and uncom-fortable, like being a child again, but not as bad as the calliope mornings of active alcoholism. The life I'd only dreamed of, based in love and service, grounded and yet expansive, required the desire and willingness to be repented. I prayed, "God, give me all I can stand, but be aware I can't stand much yet because I'm so pissed off."

Then my son became a father when he was nineteen. It had not been in the cards for either of us. It was hard sometimes, weirder than fiction, so as soon as my grandson, Jax, was big enough, we starting taking trips to the zoo. He was never afraid of the carousel or the music, not once, and I learned to savor these times, this menagerie. It was part of my being repented, to show up places where I might have been afraid, like the zoo, and in a marriage. The Bethesda man's disability had embittered him, and he wanted to be healed on his terms only—by being lowered into the water. Then when he *was* healed, he was an ingrate.

I get it: all my sober friends know that any of us alcoholics worth our salt would betray our best friends for the sake of our addiction. The man at the healing waters was addicted to having things his way.

Doesn't sound like anyone I know, except for maybe the pedicuring minister, and me.

The minister believes that only people who re-pent and become fundamentalist Christians will

be saved. He basks in his certainty. I bask in mine,
that he is wrong. Friends save us, service to others
saves us. Books, nature, community, and music
save us. Still, I find the minister kind of touching.
He just needs to be repented. Maybe I will go back
and be so kind that this will help repent him.
Kindness anywhere gives me hope; it changes us.
Those who were sober never gave up on anyone—I
am exhibit A—and so I don't, either, ever.

But repent? *Moi?* I've got bigger fish to fry, with
my grandson about to start sixth grade; getting
ready for the next election; weirdness abounding;
one gutted world to help save; and co-creation of
one life for two people to live, autonomous and
merged. And anyway, I've been successfully repented.

So while I do not expect to get over much, I
know that my motley, beloved friends and I have
only a short time together left on this merry-go-
round, as it spins around the sun, rises and falls.
At the same time, these friends are all sort of a
marvelous mess: perfect and neurotic, driven and
gentle, self-centered and crazily generous, fully
alive and probably on their way out. They are
chipped and slightly faded works of art, and they
are the exact horse I've longed for, all my life.

Four

✦

SNAIL
HYMN

✦

I continue to wait patiently for several people to come to me begging for my forgiveness before they die—a change that is about as likely to happen for me as any breakthrough for the turkey in the old *New Yorker* cartoon marching with a placard that says "Repent!"

I'm waiting for one of the most damaging boyfriends of my life, with whom I broke up twenty years ago. (Still waiting.) Others: My poor mother, who was both a terrorist and a child. My father, a womanizer, who taught me to disrespect her and therefore myself. Both are dead, so not much hope (but still). George W. Bush. (I have pretty much given up on Clarence Thomas.) And another is me.

People like to say that we cannot forgive others until we forgive ourselves. Isn't that nice? People like to say all sorts of stupid bumper-sticker things that aren't true and that in fact can be shaming, such as that God never gives us more than we can handle. What a crock. (My friend Mary says, in response, that you should never give God any idea of how much you might be able to bear. Lowball Him, like a trainer at the gym who thinks you might be able to lift a heavier weight. Say that you injured your lower back doing that once. Hint at liability.)

I have forgiven most people who have hurt me or behaved atrociously to those I love, although there is *one* extended family member who (I'm positive) makes Jesus sick to His stomach. Yet from time to time, I forgive myself for being a bad forgiver. Forgiving ourselves is the advanced practice—it's Senior Lifesaving.

It is a tricky business. The comedian Cameron Esposito put it well: "I remember a close friend's mom asking me if I really felt comfortable wearing a swimsuit next to her daughter's much more slender body. I was eight. When you are a little kid, you can't protect yourself from this shit. You think the shit is you."

You thought the shit was you, all through the years, and droplets got trapped in various chambers of memory. Even with years of recovery or therapy—after making amends and working on self-acceptance and even experiencing patchy moments of transcendence, after having mostly forgiven ourselves for not caring, for ambition, materialism, wasting time, and gluttony—it can still be exacting. The fear of your defective na-ture resurfaces, the way chicken pox resurfaces as shingles. But at some point you realize that we all have dual citizenship here, perfect and neurotic. Ram Dass said you have to remember only two things: your Buddha nature and your Social Secu-rity number. And wonderfully, there is not enough memory to keep track of every old grievance. This is the grace of age. So one forgives as one is able, except for maybe those two or three special con-tenders and oneself.

Each full act of forgiveness and even each partial act is not only a miracle, but a prize of re-demption, as with books of S&H Green Stamps. But instead of a toaster, you get a unit of peace. Each act of forgiveness gives us more awareness of the beauty that surrounds us and of the friendly light inside, the tiny and usually ignored part that hasn't been faked, cheapened, or exploited. It is an infinitesimally small point of light—like when our ancient TVs were turning off—and eternity, the world in a blade of grass.

It has taken me years to have tastes of this. It takes so long to grow up. I hate that.

Forgiveness, I know now, is maturity. Mercy is maturity. It's slow release, like certain medicines. It's incremental, like traveling along the spiral chambers of a nautilus.

I once brought my Sunday school kids a nautilus shell, because if you want to help kids fall in love with God, help them fall in love with nature. My friend Mark, who also teaches Sunday school, taught me that, and it is one of only a few great lessons I can teach.

He also showed me a way to help my kids with their terror of what we've done to the earth. "Ah!" he said, excitedly, when I asked for guidance, as if I had come to the right place. "First teach them how we live with sin."

I nodded Hasidically. Then I asked, "How *do* we live with sin?"

I sinned so much in my twenties and early thirties, until I got sober, when I moved from moral turpitude to the simple cloth-coat sins of inertia, judgment, and morbid reflection. The women who helped me get sober in the eighties, when I told them how bad my behavior had been, waved their hands dismissively and said, "Oh, me too." This began to relieve me of my bottomless shame. They said, Leave it alone. Don't pick at it. Let it heal. Don't have any affairs today.

Sin is not just affairs, or porn shops, or drug cartels. It is also the ignorance and brokenness of the world, extreme self-centeredness, hoarding wealth, using others as objects, not caring.

Mark said that to teach the kids how we live with sin, take them to a beach. So I did. (Never disobey Sunday school teachers. They will fuck with you.)

The beach was cluttered and littered with plastic bottles and crap of every kind. We walked around and saw what we saw—damage to this gorgeous beach, what human behavior had wrought. I invited the kids to experience sorrow, disgust, and anger. I asked them how it made them feel.

It made them feel sad, scared, hopeless. So we cleaned up one part of the beach as much as we could. Mark had recommended that we bring back some of the garbage. Bring in the ugly and the sad, along with sand and shells. So we brought in some trash and some treasures. Then, this being Sunday school and not biology, we laid it all beneath the arms of the cross, because then it is held; it became part of the bigger story, the bigger reality. Not just the crud from one section of one ruined beach, but a variety of things from what was now a cleaner beach, a beach loved and held by caring people, kids who care. You admit that the ugly and repulsive and sad do exist, and they are happening, but we don't have to believe it is us, and run away from it, from the cross, from the beach, from our own crooked hearts.

This is how we live with sin, sickness, and a world on fire.

Taking kids outside to love God in nature is just about the most Jesusy thing we can do. Jesus was nearly always outside with His disciples or alone with the stars. To take kids to a beach, even one that is littered, is to bring them to an altar, a big one, surrounded by the blue-gray ocean billowing outward like a skirt, flecked with sunlight, like foil or diamonds.

But the nautilus class was at the end of summer and was scheduled to be a short service, and it didn't make sense to take the kids to the beach. Only one girl was in the Sunday school classroom that day. So I brought the beach to her, as a bag of shrimp chips, a Hawaiian Punch from the church pantry, and a few nautilus shells. Far be it from me to dive into such a New Age cliché, although even my bad-attitude atheist friends have to admit that the nautilus is mathematically interesting and beautiful, the inside especially. But I could show the girl only the outside, and a photo of the inside.

Each of the nautilus shell chambers, starting at the very inside of the spiral, is incrementally bigger than the one before, until there is the outermost space where the mollusk lives. It's the creature's living quarters, its crib. The chambers hold gas extracted during respiration, for buoyancy and propulsion. The nautilus, protected in the final chamber, is both inside and yet connected to the outside, to water and food. Even my atheist friends admit, too, that this is a good metaphor for the safe space that's in each of us, where there is relief from anxiety and self-consciousness, where there is room to breathe, to settle in, settle down, mull things over without anyone's hot breath on our necks.

The girl handled the shell with due reverence. It was all curves and stripes, reminiscent of animal stripes, asymmetrical and good for camouflage. She traced the curve with her small fingers, as you might stroke a cat's back. Nature seems to know that the curve is the best way to be, smooth and flowing, without any sharp edges. A shield is curved, our ribs are curved; there can be protection in a curve. You don't get so easily smashed into by curves as you do by objects with sharp sides. And everything in the curve is balanced, which is so rare.

I was not going to teach the usual message of the spiral, that we can grow from the innermost kernel of understanding into expansion.

Well, maybe I would, just for a second, in passing.

A spiral is the ultimate statement of the harmonious. It does not grow in fits, starts, and back steps, but rather, in a flow. And chambers can be sacred, because they invite you in, even as they protect you, perhaps somewhat like your parents were supposed to, and possibly meant to.

The girl turned the shell over in her hand to study the opening. It was small, unlike a conch, but still she held it to her ear to hear the song of the universe, elegant and playful, like Bach with a girl-group backup, centered in harmonies.

We took some time to study the photograph of the shell's inside chambers, the swirl of its expansion from barely visible to roomy. It has an exquisite, perpetually steady rhythm, like the ocean or our heartbeats.

The last detail I wanted to point out, before we had the sacrament of shrimp chips, was that when everything keeps expanding, there is still room in all of us for breath, which is what keeps us alive.

What is nature sharing with us? If something is allowed to grow the way it was designed to, it works. When we try to get it to conform to the supposedly more efficient image we have of it, we get grotesqueries, imbalances. When we try to get difficulties to conform to our way of thinking, we often push them toward being fancier, and thus absurd. We strip away the grace of what is real, and true, and maybe even lovely.

My Sunday school class and I had only ten minutes left, so we couldn't get into the Fibonacci spiral, the mathematical sequence we find in pine cones, seed heads, and the nautilus. The outside of a pineapple or seeds in a sunflower, for instance, are arranged in uniform, efficient spirals so that the seeds in the center don't get crowded and squished and the ones outside don't fall off. This sort of exactitude, balance, and order are what we humans rarely experience but so long for.

I note that, coincidentally, the designs *I* didn't design seem to work much more often than mine.

Something about the spiral and other kinds of

curves makes you want to throw your arm outward and around as in the port de bras of a ballerina, with a deep breath and a long sweep of your arms, so you become a curve, too.

"And then what makes it sacred," I told the girl, "is the life inside, its being—the snail!" I was so moved by what I had just said that I clutched my chest.

"Hmmm," she said, opening the bag of chips.

"It breathes, it has babies, it scooches around through jet propulsion. It has memory. It can live twenty years." I paused for effect. "Brother snail!"

When I got home from church, I went online and ordered a split nautilus shell for her, so she could see the coil of chambers, how it (and maybe we) grow.

Forgiveness grows like this, too.

One of the women I hurt most in my twenties, named Esther, began to forgive me thirty-two years ago, when I reached out to her via snail mail. I tried to make amends to her for having had a drunken and sporadic affair with her husband.

I had been sober a year when I expressed deep contrition, through a long letter, as I could not face her. I had not seen her or her family for five years. I did not expect her to forgive me for what I had done to her and, by extension, her children, but sober friends thought that that was her business.

She wrote back right away and said that for her as a Jew, forgiveness was a duty, or a mitzvah, and she had forgiven me long before. She hoped that I was able to stay sober and that, because my guilt had alienated me from humanity, God, and myself, over time I could forgive myself.

I put down her letter and cried into my sinner hands.

Over time, I did forgive myself, in a piecemeal way, a bit here and there, because I wanted the reward of a lighter life, looser chains. When memories of my sexual behavior arose, I felt sick and sad about it, and then I tried to leave it alone. Some days went better than others. I tried to let it heal, slowly learned to trust myself again and to care gently for myself, much of the time.

But the guilt of those injuries, to women and children, never quite left me. Not too long ago, I told a close friend about Esther's husband, and other women's men, hanging my head, heavy with remorse. My friend was near tears—for *me*.

"I feel such compassion for that young woman, who had to get those men and be chosen by them to feel alive, of value, for a moment's respite," she said. "Because living inside her skin and head hurt too much."

The deepest part of me flickered. I saw that skinny young woman, drinking, smoking, shy but flirting, loved by all but by none where it mattered.

And then the craziest thing happened: Thirty-plus years after our letters, Esther appeared in one of my writing workshops. We hugged, beaming, me with my heart in my throat. She was still a hippie, a beautiful, decades-older version of herself (poor dear, how had that happened?). She had a gift for me. It was a dime, a nickel, and three pennies, bound with Scotch tape, stacked into a sticky tower, like a child might make.

"Eighteen is a spiritual number in Judaism," she said, "so we Jews give gifts of money in multiples of eighteen, as blessings."

One blessing she gave me was metallic, chunky, and sticky, another was holy. She spent the day with me and 150 others, one of many, scribbling and laughing in one another's company. You can't get there from where either of us was. There is no straight route. Life is so inefficient that way, and it doesn't really work for me at all. It works by spirals, squiggles, and ink blots, looping back and over and around like a child's Möbius strip.

The experience left me longing to be more like her, to evolve toward deeper goodness and courage with the time I have left. Jesus is big on people evolving, and all organisms have an innate tendency to evolve toward improvement. I seemed to be the outlier. But I now felt the call to face old hostilities head-on, to begin forgiving everyone unconditionally, as the greatest blessing I could give myself. I would get on the phone to the bad boyfriend, the skeevy relative. I'd be the Mary Lou Retton of mercy.

Sad to say, the urge left by the time I got back home. I took a nap instead.

These days the same old slide show still plays from time to time in my head, of the people I hope will come begging for my forgiveness, but it plays without as much tooth or perseverance. I have learned in my third third of life that forgiveness is a grace: you can't force it, you can only set the mechanism to Receive. I have evolved to the point where mine is at least now set to Vacillate. Sometimes when I am filled with hostility, usually for people in the public sphere, I carry Esther's tower of taped coins in my mental pocket as a dowsing rod, to suss out any breeze of forgiveness that is looking for a place to roost. Pick me, pick me! I want to contribute to the aquifer that runs underneath our communities, of people who have made peace with others against all odds, because that groundwater helps restore and sustain life. It did in South Africa's Truth and Reconciliation Commission, in Esther, and even in me. (That many of my forgiven are dead should not detract from the heroic and inspiring work it took for me to forgive them.) I don't have a clue how to forgive the most destructive people who have impacted my life and my family's, and I don't have much to go on, beyond my faith in the divine and in Esther's eighteen cents. Oh, and some magical snail shells. Sometimes the brown bands on the outer case of a nautilus shell almost join together in the center, like tiger stripes, or the fingertips in the Sistine Chapel seen from the ground, just missing each other, and the margins between the sworls waver mystically as if under water.

Five

LUNCH-MONEY
FAITH

My best friends are exhausted, furious, and afraid. It is not a charming combination. I show them Esther's eighteen-cent tower as proof of healing and evolution, but some days are just way too long and upsetting for them. I would get a fresh new batch of friends if not for the fact that half the time I have all these feelings, too. This is partly because we have accidentally gotten so much older, and also because of the enervating nature of these cruel times. Our adrenaline spikes often, to keep up. We are sometimes with cherished friends who have gotten scary diagnoses, or we sit beside them at memorial services, all while glaciers calve huge babies on our screens and our short-term memories dissolve like Pop Rocks. Jeremiah said, "The harvest is past, the summer is ended, and we are not saved," and waiting for salvation has worn us out.

We had our money on special investigations, oncologists, clinical trials, the radical young climate activists, grown kids straightening out, and lots of people blew our minds with sincere efforts, doggedness, or expertise. Yet not only were we not saved, things are more dire, and friends more manic, drained, and stuck. This sucks, to use the theological term. But the other day my friend Terri Tate said something that is turning things around for me.

She looked bleary and clenched at the door of our church, where she is the usher, as she collected the programs to recycle. A successful writer in her early seventies, she survived a basically unsurvivable cancer twenty-five years ago, and now has two grown sons and a crazily loved teenage granddaughter. I thought she had a migraine, so I asked her if she was okay. She shook her head and sighed. "I have made a life and career of being a good sport," she said. "And I am worn out." All I could think to do in the moment was to agree.

Me too. I am sick and tired of being such a good sport and worker bee, chin up and adorably ironic, while we notice how much worse things have grown. My friends and I have dark conversations now about the end of democracy and climate catastrophe, and people's voices trail off. At one dear friend's party, everyone started talking about the best ways to commit suicide until the friend's wife started crying because the conversation was ruining her party. What a big baby. Yet each day the data stream is even more bizarre and disheartening. Terri said what everyone is feeling: It is too much. You steadfastly love and serve everyone, see people through tribulation, savor the relief, and give thanks. Then boing—a new setback. It's like tucking an octopus into bed at night: new arms keep popping out.

"How can I serve you?" I asked. Terri requested a lively story of burnout and hope.

I was going to teach my Sunday school kids a good one that day, so I shared it with Terri.

We would begin with the only known sighting of God's butt.

When Moses asks to see God on Mount Sinai (or Horeb) in Exodus 32, God answers, "No one can see my face and live." This is a common notion in religions about God's overpowering transcendence. Instead, God says to Moses, "Go inside a cave and I will cover you with my hand; after I go by, you can come out and see my back." Any child hearing this, and in fact bad people like me, would turn that into seeing God's behind. Beavis and Butt-Head do theology.

One has to wonder what God's behind looks like. If you see God as the old bearded man in the sky, the butt would almost certainly resemble Grandaddy's, which is—no offense—not exactly celestial. My friend Father Jim says God's behind must be more like Brad Pitt's in *Thelma and Louise*, only shinier. This insight cheered up Terri somewhat.

This idea got me interested at some point in Elijah on the same mountain, six hundred or so years later.

Elijah's situation was pretty gnarly: Israel was deeply divided into those following the God of Abraham and Moses, and those worshipping the ancient Canaanite god Baal. Elijah was trying to persuade people to abide by the covenant with God and do what was later codified by Micah, and convince them that God really wished that they would act justly, love mercy, and walk humbly with God. (Although by then Micah had figured out something that Elijah hadn't, which is that violence wasn't the answer.) The king, Ahab, was insane, cruel, and narcissistic—which does not remind me of anyone else I can think of—but Elijah was pretty cranky, too. He prophesied to Ahab and his mad queen, Jezebel, that there would be a drought so catastrophic that not even dew would form. Yikes. Also, Elijah and his men had slit the throats of all of Baal's prophets, which you don't hear about during National Brotherhood Week. Ahab also threatened to kill him, so Elijah wisely took off for the wilderness.

He was severely depressed as he lay under a broom brush, and he prayed that he might die. He said, "I have had enough."

This is what the folks in recovery mean by Step One, where you admit you've crashed and burned and have run out of any more good ideas.

Then Elijah slept.

This existential exhaustion is everywhere we look these days in our world, our nation, and in our beloved, maybe especially in our teenagers and our very closest friends. At one end of the spectrum are those in the throes of lifelong forward thrust, who are focused on goals that turn out to be meaningless, greyhounds at the track who've caught the mechanical rabbit of prestige, and at the other end are people with slow-motion tragedies unfolding in their lives.

Terri and I share a close friend in both recovery and church whose twenty-two-year-old son has incurable brain cancer. So once again one wonders: How on earth do we sustain any optimism at all, not give up on life, and stay more or less okay one day at a time in the face of such a devastating reality and prognosis? I asked our friend.

"I just can't give up," she said, "and under the fear and terror there's something that won't let me. Also," she added, "what is the option? I live with a level of mess, of what I can't control, of what I don't think I can bear. Yet I love my life. I'm grateful for my kids, and all of you, my faith in goodness and love, and certain Jedi mind skills that come with getting older. And the beauty of our backyard, and the mountain. My dogs and cats. The secret of people in my position is that we do what we have to do. Sometimes I'm numb, sometimes wired and exhausted, like the Energizer bunny in very old age. Sometimes I am okay. P.S., my definition of 'okay' is constantly changing. Okay today is that my son is making art with really kind people. Okay is right now."

She told me not long ago, "I'm not suicidal, but sometimes I wish I was dead." This is the point beyond exhaustion, when you can't see how you'll ever fill up again. And then she does, through what she calls lunch-money faith: nothing dramatic, and just enough.

Another friend of mine once gave a spiritual retreat on rising up, on renewal and second winds in these catastrophic times. One woman who participated, who works with kids who have AIDS, came all the way from Africa. My friend talked all morning about filling back up, about energy reserves that are released by curiosity and (paradoxically) service. Then he helped each student take a nap, like in kindergarten. He had bought fifty beautiful Mexican blankets for the students. The woman from Africa was furious with him for wasting her time—she had come so far and wanted the teaching. He tried to soothe her, but she went with her blanket to the back of the room. Everyone lay down, stretched out or curled up, closed their eyes or spaced out, and rested. The woman came over after the nap and told him, "I slept. I dreamed. I'm beyond exhausted. I hadn't even known that."

. . .

A few weeks after our wedding, Neal and I were at a spiritual retreat on Maui, where I had already given two talks and sat on two panels before large audiences. I was in our hotel room alone, gazing out to sea, when I had a vision, as in "Your old will have visions, and your young will dream dreams." But it was not a beautiful honeymoon vision of flower girls and my grandson bearing our rings. I saw myself out past the waves, swimming toward the horizon, beyond my ability to make it back. I was just so, so tired.

I did the only thing I know to do: I said it, I told the truth. I went and found Neal, and even though I worried he would have buyer's remorse, I told him, and I cried. Ninety percent of the time, this is the solution: Tell it. Cry if you can. If you can't, sit in a dejected posture, hunched over, and stay with this awhile. It will shift, and become less acute.

He listened, and he got it. He did not try to fix me or cheer me up, so he could have a cute, fun wife again. He listened. Then we went to the buffet and overate together. (He is a keeper.)

Ah, food. In our story, it's shortcake covered with berries and whipped cream. In Elijah's, an angel wakes him up for a hearth cake, as he needs to eat. I love this so much. You pay twenty-five dollars to hear one of my heroes, Thich Nhat Hanh, say: "When you walk, just walk." You think: I paid good money for this? Notice your feet as they connect to the earth? Left foot, right foot, breathe? Crazy.

A hearth cake would have been plain fried bread, not like some nice Starbucks oatcake with dried apricots and glazed pecans, but bread for the journey, nourishment to get Elijah to where he needed to be, a strengthening food to get him back to the mountain where the covenant was first made—where we will see God's majestic behind and maybe hear God's whispers of presence.

Where can we hear any whispers in the cacophony, behind the drama and trauma and fever dreams of our era? With our phones to our ears, life and our minds frequently feel like casinos now. There is no sun, no pocket of quiet, there don't seem to be exits, and the reception is terrible. Connection to anything real, to the ancient, to the mystical, to the moment, is weak, so there is bound to be existential exhaustion.

The great Buddhist teacher Jack Kornfield told me about his forest teacher decades ago in

Laos, telling him that his thoughts, memories, and projections were just movies playing in the theater of his mind all the time—romantic movies, adventure movies, horror movies, travelogues, and so forth. The central question was: Who is watching all these movies?

Who is the watcher, deeply inside?

Greta Thunberg, the young radical climate activist, calls on us to dig deep beneath the noise and to focus as if our house is on fire, because it is. She says she does not want our hope for her generation's future—she wants our panic. She and other young activists hit some kind of low note for me, one that holds us up, as do the Black Lives Matter marchers, as did the young gun-control activists in Parkland, Florida, like timpani at the back of the orchestra. Maybe this is not what you are listening for—you love the clarinet, or the cello—but underneath is a low thrum. I'm listening for Greta now, rather than for my generation's brilliant ironic literary lights who explain that there is really no hope. I read one recently in *The New Yorker*, a famous novelist, and I saw a withered, brittle man, small of soul. Then Greta, illumined, spoke fiercely at the United Nations, looking the heart of darkness directly in the eye and calling for an international awakening and a strike.

Most scientists now don't think we can stop climate catastrophe. (One of our climatologist friends is raising her daughter with stories of single women, raising her not to have children.) But I am not a scientist. I'm a potentially violent grandmother, and so I hope we can, and I do what little I can, with conviction. These hard jobs are exactly what we have done throughout history. We stopped Hitler, we stopped smallpox, we stopped DDT. And at my most self-destructive, I stopped me; or at any rate, something good stopped me.

I was stuck in staying one step ahead, tightly wrapped, fairly successful with hunched shoulders, filled with fears and tears, exhausted but the ultimate good sport, always cheerful or at least conversational. Sometimes we have to get cancer or have a heart attack to stop the train of wired meaninglessness, to stop faking or stuffing it all back down. But I got lucky. A few people asked how I was, when the answer was clear, and they would tell me how therapy or religion or Weight Watchers or recovery had helped them begin to heal from whatever was killing their souls. I'd think: Look, this is very nice, but I know the ending. I'm happy for you, but I really need to get back to work. Then I couldn't even summon the confidence to sit down and work. My mind wanted me dead, but it always settled for getting me drunk.

Elijah couldn't go back to work, because Ahab wanted him dead. So I went to bed, while Elijah, fortified by the hearth cake, walked through the desert to Mount Sinai, where his community's roots were—where Moses saw God's tuchus and got the Ten Commandments.

Here Elijah meets God, not in the usual special effects of the Exodus tradition, not the roar of hurricane or flames, but in a still, small voice. Jewish and Christian writers have seen in this a reminder of the importance of contemplation, of quietness, of listening.

"Why are you here?" God asks. What a crazy question!

I am not sure how I might answer that. Growing up, learning. I am slowly making my way from a hypnotized engine of delusion and self-obsession to being a bit more real, a smidge more alive more often. I'll take it. I am learning to live more often in reckless love. I used to pray like Flip Wilson— "I'm about to pray—anyone need anything?" Now

I often just say to God, "Hi. Help me feel You in this with me." I am learning to listen for fragments of truth from any wisdom tradition that are usually found in stories and, like Elijah, for whispers that I am not alone in this.

Some days go better than others.

On bad days, I text my friend Janine and say, "I hate everyone and all of life. These are end days, children." She says she is glad I reached out, and then I am better. We cruise for hearth cakes, and if we can't find any, T-shirts at Target, M&M's, or chai help.

There are many kinds of food.

My friends are the low note that hold me. Love is the whisper of wire drum-brushes. And while everyone has to make a living and show up for family, listening is optional: you have to make a conscious decision to begin listening harder.

Whether it's Mount Sinai, a pasture, a library, the creek down the road, aliveness (or whatever you want to call it) the song is above us, around us, within us. We transcend the incessant and wearying yammer of bullshit. Transcendence means you go from judgment, separation from life and yourself, to feeling at one-ish with the universe. We hook into something bigger than we are, truer than the self-serving stories we make up about life and ourselves.

I love Terri's fabulous old soul of a grand-daughter, Georgie, who sometimes comes to church. She is already mature and down-to-earth yet also very cool, so with her I try to focus on the mystical side of things. (She adores me but I be-lieve she finds me a little cosmic, though she man-ages to restrain herself from actually patting me on the arm.) I try to help teenagers learn to pay attention—attention as caffeine. (The most atten-tive people I know are birdwatchers. They are less sleepy as a whole than the general population.) Look up and around at the pine trees, I tell them. Look at crows, look at all the people who want to help teenagers get both centered and dreamier. I urge them to be in places where they can receive. This is usually outside, or in a room where they can create. I try to help them see how alive they feel when they are writing whatever they actually want to write, instead of what their teachers want them to, and recognize how less tired they feel when they are outside painting.

Learning to bear that aliveness, that fresh-ness, is why I am here, what I am in it for, and what can spritz me out of the casino. When we study

Elijah, I ask the Sunday school kids, Why are *you* here?

"Our parents dragged us," they say, but they secretly love me and the other teacher, Bonnie, because we talk about real things, and serve snacks. They see us as a relatively animating way to spend time until they can connect with their friends again. More than anything else, they love their friends. They sleep with their phones so they can check messages all night: Are you there? Are you still my friend? They love escape—on their phones, on the web. They also love escaping within, spacing out, sleeping, free for a few stolen hours.

Why are they here in the world? To grow up, to learn about life, who they are, to come to understand what is real. Others will teach them how to get ahead, mask fear, push past fatigue, and pretend to be doing fine at all times, but here in Sunday school, we can help them discover who they are, how to be fully human, warts and vulnerability and all.

Why am I here? To love this dumb old day. Oh, if only I could remember this.

God tells Elijah to go back to the roiling land of Ahab and Jezebel with his message, the same message people in 12 Step recovery carry, that there is a way to peace. And so Elijah sets off, half dead not long before, now renewed. He must have dreaded leaving the mountain. Most of these prophets were introverts. Jesus definitely was. He's never really doing all that much, if you think about it. He doesn't even tell His own stories. He'd be fired from most churches today. He's in a world of great fear, there's evil, violence, and need all around him, so He often finds He needs time alone—in silence, in the desert, on the mountain, on the beach, beneath the stars—to get strong and patient enough to go back and face Peter's lame and endless questions for the tenth time: "Is now when we get to be in charge? Is now when we take over?"

Even now we aren't in charge of much, and it is exhausting to believe or pretend we are. The best we can do is to help the poor, get some rest, help the pets at mealtime, observe the rules of health and safety during the virus. Watching the ways we try to be in charge can help us get our sense of humor back, and laughter is a holy and subversive battery charge.

Elijah's story ends with him making a great friend for life: Elisha, his successor, by whom he is loved and from whom he is inseparable until he rises in flames at the moment of his death.

I saw Terri at church the other day. She stood up straight and saluted me at the door when she saw me, which is very silly for an usher and which I kindly pointed out to her. I asked how she was, and she said sometimes she still has a feeling of deep melancholy, the sadness of life passing, her baby granddaughter now learning to drive. But most of the time she feels a grateful sadness, that life is so beautiful and full of wonder though so short. She listens for truth and stories she can pass along. She listens for whispers.

By the same token, she and I got to hear glorious noise that day. A woman who has been at our church for forty years, seven years before I first arrived drunk, has a voice that goes way beyond actual sound. She grew up in the Deep South. Both her sons have been in prison, and she has very little in the worldly sense. But her faith and the voice with which she sings make her rich and give her the second wind for which we all yearn. She doesn't take credit for it. She didn't create it. Her voice reminds me of a didgeridoo, breath carried through a long, long tunnel. She always shows up to church exhausted, as she typically

works six days a week, but she opens her mouth,
throat, and heart, and everything that is deep inside the exhaustion and pain she carries—love,
praise, her ancestors, nature—lends her the notes
she needs to go on.

Six

+

LIGHT
BREEZES

+

P raise songs were not a part of my childhood. We were too sophisticated for that.
We didn't believe in an invisible and loving companion. We believed in Dad, who did not
love Mom, so life was scary. Dread was my governess growing up.

She kept me alive. I didn't run out into the
street, didn't talk to strangers, didn't sass, wiped
front to back, minded my manners and teachers,
stayed on my toes, did well in school. She would
have made an excellent character in the Old
Testament—"The fear of God is the beginning of
wisdom"—although as my parents were atheist,
she would have had to tone down the blood atone-
ment. It was into her arms that I retreated from
the emotional land mines and overwhelm of the
world and the dining table, and from the secret if

occasional experience that deep inside me was an infinite, untrammeled soul.

My parents did not hire her to keep me small and obedient, to keep me separate from all of you and all of life and most of me. I hired her. I was three or four. She was my most reliable companion, always there for me, like God in a bad mood.

She looked like a tall, thin Greek goddess you wouldn't want to tangle with.

Dread taught me how to succeed and why it mattered, how to survive the caffeinated neglect of my home life, the bullying on the blacktop, the equally fraught states of isolation and intimacy. She kept me in line, helped me to be someone everyone would like. She got me to where I am today.

It has always been hard for her to let go of me and for me to let go of her, because I might die or disappoint my parents, now long dead. It does seem she has loosened her grip somewhat in the third third. She is still my default in fearful times like these, when I am stunned by the horrors of the powers that be, by the UN climate report and the pandemic, by dying friends who are younger than I, sometimes much younger. Even though I know from God, from precious community, and from various calming spiritual practices that heal

and hold during catastrophic weirdness, she re-
fuses to cede control. Even though I know the extreme hardships Dread and I have already come
through—I know that somehow, against all odds,
we somehow always seem to—she steps in to offer
her cranky thoughts on just how utterly fucked
and inadequate things are . . . beginning with me.

Dread is having a field day with my recent
marriage. So many things could destroy it if I
don't play my cards exactly right, day by day. Neal
may have a second family tucked away in the sub-
urbs, or early pancreatic cancer. He may discover
how pathetic I actually am, how damaged, how
much I am faking. But even if any of these are
true, the love of my community has always been
and will always be enough to keep me afloat, and
then it will transform me. That is a point on which
the governess and I disagree.

For instance, Donald Trump was still presi-
dent that day after Easter, which was not ideal for
old lefty me and which constantly threatened to
sink my spirit. But the day after that first Easter,
some two thousand years ago, Herod was still
king, Caesar was still in Rome, the chief priests
were still chief priests. Yet the twelve men who
followed Jesus were utterly transformed, as were

some women. This could not be denied, or the stones would have cried out. So with my fading memory, I try to remember.

The great dread of our childhood was nuclear annihilation, but that would have amounted to only a few random continents, child's play compared to what we face now. We ducked under desks in grade school to avoid radiation and giggled. Our parents were in a panic during the Cuban Missile Crisis, but again, that was child's play compared with the dead zone and bickering of their marriage, plus the terror of possible divorce. In junior high, we didn't know about Greenland's melting ice sheet, but we knew that we had bad hair, or needed glasses, braces, breasts, self-confidence, and maybe a joint or a nice cool beer.

Now looming behind all of life, monolithically, is the rising, terrifying heat.

If Dread is not still right there at my side, she's there in the wings, humming her hymns, drumming her fingers, knowing there is always a place for her in my heart. Life will push her call button. Neal might have left me at the altar, or it could have rained and wrecked my hair. So Dread is there with any strange sound the car makes while I'm driving on the freeway, or when anyone I love has to do a blood test. I've put a lot on her plate. She can work with any smell, news, or ache.

The last few times that my aging dog has had routine blood tests at the vet's, to monitor medication she's on, she has shown increasingly elevated liver enzymes. The vet explained that this could be cancer, but that there were also some treatable explanations. She recommended an ultrasound to make sure there were no masses in Lady Bird's liver, and also added that I should stay off the internet.

And I did, until quite late that night. I waited until Neal had fallen asleep. We had been married only a month and I did not want him to worry about how much I continue to worry. He might not have wanted a cute new wife whose mind is often in air-traffic-control mode.

Maybe "cute new wife" is a bit of a misnomer, although people like to say you're only as old as you feel. Isn't that nice? We both feel good physically, blessed with good health, but it's funny how much time the two of us spend at the doctor's for such young and active people. We're like the car your uncle sold to you for a hundred dollars when you came home from college, a Chevy Malibu station wagon. Hey, no major dents and it still runs.

Maybe a few random issues. Name one body system, and I can assure you that one of us has been to see the doctor about it recently. One of us—and I won't name names—had to pee into a cup in our bathroom every few hours for a whole day, and then collect it in a plastic jug. Does that sound very romantic to you? Is that something from *Brides* magazine?

So eyes, hips, hearing, cholesterol, blood pressure, feet. Problems with all of these are par for the course, along with the memory lapses, which are the source of the greatest dread. And, well, bigger and bigger memory lapses, until they are pretty worrisome, if not occasionally terrifying. I couldn't remember Joe Biden's first name the other day. But then my friends and I compare our latest little moments of forgetfulness, reassure one another that we've done it, too, and then some. Oh well— the keys, the phone, the glasses that are on top of our heads. We get to—have to—finally release the perfectionism and expectations, expectations being resentments under construction. We can't get bogged down in this stupid stuff. It's actually a miracle just to be here at all, with a few truly great friends, and to keep muddling through, grateful if sometimes perplexed.

I was pretty sure the ultrasound would show that Lady Bird was just fine, and that life was, too. No reason to worry.

Then I took a fistful of my dog's medicine.

Every morning I give her two Benadryl pills for her allergies, hidden in cheese, and one other tablet for her old-lady incontinence. This is usually something I can manage, until I am rocketing around trying to do too many things at once, in which case I forget, and she pees on the couch, or I drop the pills while slamming my hand in the refrigerator door. This always reminds me of something from about twenty years ago, when my son was nine, and I was dragging him behind me along the docks in San Francisco on my way to do a live radio interview. Holding a stack of papers, a heavy purse slung over my shoulder, I inevitably dropped the papers, which blew in the wind onto the bay, the pilings, and (I like to imagine) some rather startled pelicans. My son stopped in his tracks and yanked on my arm. "Mom," he said fretfully, "you're carrying too much and you're going too fast."

These were also the conditions when I took the dog's medicine.

These are, in fact, the conditions of life a lot of

the time: carrying too much in my mind, going too fast, caring for so many people, trying to get just one more thing done before I have to be somewhere—don't forget to stop for toothpaste and graph paper!—pummeled by the data stream of terrifying developments and the latest news on global warming and COVID-19. So racing around with Lady Bird's pills in my hand, I took my eyes off the ball and flung the pills down my throat.

The second I swallowed them, I said out loud to God, "Please don't let me have just taken the dog's pills."

God sighed.

I was already having a late start getting to an appointment in the East Bay, so I just got in the car and called the vet as I drove. I explained what had happened and said, "Oh well, hah hah, you must get this all the time." She said, very nicely, "No, not really."

She added that the dog's incontinence meds had been banned by the FDA for human use twenty years earlier, so I really needed to call my doctor.

I stopped to get a double espresso to counter-act the Benadryl, and then called my prayer part-ner, who happens to be a doctor at Stanford. She told me I needed to watch for signs of hypertension and a racing heartbeat, but that the odds were good that I would live. "Maybe take it a little easy today, until the Benadryl wears off," she said.

She is twenty years younger than I. She did not question my operating heavy machinery while on antihistamines, or suggest I get a complete cognitive workup. She didn't think I was going to have a stroke or a massive heart attack. She just said I'd be fine and to have a blessed day. What a nut. Yet her encouraging words were a gentle breeze on my poor mind, and this is the work of the Holy Spirit and our operating instructions, to be cooling breezes to sad or worried people, including ourselves, in this sometimes hot stuffy joint.

I had a whole sunny day ahead of me. My wonderful new married life!

Then, unfortunately, twenty minutes later the symptoms of heart attack started. They began with a speeding pulse like a submachine gun, my heart pounding out of my chest as in a cartoon where a heart-shaped fist in a boxing glove is punching out from within a body. This was going to look terrible in my obituary. People would shake their heads sadly: "After all she'd come through! All those early deaths and years of alcoholism—and then to die like this. Not to sound harsh, but dying of dog meds makes a mockery of her whole life."

The governess appeared, quiet as the grave, as is her wont and her domain, pretending her job is to keep me from dying, when actually it is to keep me from living, at least outside her control. We share the worry that I am secretly a loser, a latent embarrassment, even back in the day when I could still sneeze or cough without tiny bladder control issues.

I clutched my beating heart, like Snagglepuss on stage playing Shakespeare, and then reached to take my pulse, at which point I finally remembered that I'd had those two extra shots of espresso.

Funny that the governess had not thought to remind me.

This time I stood up to her. I rose like a mother whose kid was being bullied, and said, "You again!"

My heart slowed down. And a few miles farther on, gratitude bloomed. Life, death, new life: I was back in the saddle again. Every time I bust the governess, I get free. We are going to save the world by repeatedly busting the dread that looms over us like a blimp, by pushing back our sleeves and distracting it with the next right step and good works. My friend Shelley has a massive, scary German shepherd who used to lunge at little dogs, even when he wore a shock collar, until she started giving him two tennis balls to carry around on our hikes. Now, with these balls in his mouth, he is way too busy, focused, and self-important to hurt anyone.

I loved that morning and the next few days, now that I had been sprung once again from the jaws of death. And Neal said I hardly piddled on the floor at all.

There's a Gospel story of a woman rising up against an intimidating authority, not some obvious bad guy we can all agree on, like a scribe or a Pharisee. She stands up to dear old Jesus. A Gentile woman who lives in the coastal regions, she seeks out an exhausted Jesus and begs him to come heal her daughter, who is vexed by a demon. He desperately needs rest, and besides, he thought until now that his divine mission included only his own people. He tells the mother, "Maybe later, when I've rested, and everyone has eaten." She rises up, because she has the gift of desperation, the g-o-d, and she cries out that even the dogs will be fed, will get the crumbs from the master's table, before her child will be tended to.

This shiksa talks back to him, and it radicalizes

him. He has insulted her in a conventionally racist way, and when she gives him back as good as she has gotten, he gets that she's right: He needs to heal her child. Her child is his child, too. All children count the same. Jesus no longer sees his mission of love and healing as exclusive to the chosen people. He all but smites his forehead: he's going to shoot the moon from here on in. That's what mother strength can do—change the world, one child at a time.

(My Jesuit friend Jim says, "It's her faith, but you could also correctly say it's her balls. I love that Jesus likes that in a woman.")

Inconveniently, I know that the mystery of grace means that our crazier leaders are the sick child, too, as precious to God as your new baby daughter, nephew, niece. We have to work with the fact of their incapacities. The alternative is to give in to the hopelessness and dread. Having never been loved has made some people hard and blind, so they lack the focus and insight to help save the earth for their grandchildren. That's life on life's terms, but we will include their grandchildren in the kids we watch out for. We always did, right? We always invited kids whose parents were drunk or absent or mentally ill to come play at our house. They were just kids to us. We fed them, gave them praise for their schoolwork. We took them camping with us. We saw their suffering, and the question always was: How will you respond? We school parents responded with inclusion and love. This can change the world, one kid's world, or maybe one world's kids. We see that happening all around us, in mentoring programs, marches and sanctuary movements, Head Start, the Special Olympics, community food pantries, and gay pride, and we can be glad in it.

But I wasn't glad the day of Lady Bird's ultrasound. It was so hot, the way it is supposed to be in late July but the way it gets these days in the spring, unnatural. They used to call days like this unseasonably hot, but now it feels like the penultimate days, the way the earth will be when my grandson will be ready to have children. It's hard not to give up, on just carpe the damn diem. But we don't give up. Science has given us unprecedented data about what is true and ways we might respond, and desperation has given us strength. We have the strength of a mother whose child is very, very sick, and there is nothing on earth more powerful. The earth is on fire, but the young are on fire, too. Boy, the young are angry at us. Good. This is what usually changes the world, although it's a new experience to be the us the young are mad at. When Kurt Vonnegut's children complained to him bitterly about how damaged the earth was, he said, "Shut up! I just got here myself."

So, yeah, it's another fine mess those in power have gotten us into. From what I see, the scientists, public health doctors, moms, grannies, and high school kids are on it.

The day of Lady Bird's ultrasound was sickeningly hot, ten degrees past sultry. A swath of cottony white dabs hung to one side of the hill, and over it a darkening, like smudged pencil, and behind it all an implacable blue with the already fierce sun blazing through. I let Lady Bird race around in the yard for a while but I quickly got too hot. I dropped her at the vet's, where the ultrasound people would need her for an hour and a half. She watched me leave, as if she knew she would never see me again, which is actually how she looks at me when I walk into another room. I got her at the pound when she was four, and she is nine now, a large brindle girl who looks like a deer with a huge head who is letting herself go. As with a lot of us in our third third, the weight has crept up on her.

When I got back in the car, I teared up with worry, pictured Lady Bird on chemo, if she had the good kind of cancer. But then I remembered the governess with two balls in her mouth, trotting around in arrogance and self-importance, and as I drove it occurred to me that I needed two tennis balls, too. Tasks bring us presence.

One ball was cleaning out the bad drawer in the kitchen. The other was premeditated sloth. Cleaning the junk drawer was fabulous, but sloth can be scary. Whenever you let your tummy out, the governess reacts. She's a kind of corset, to hold the body of you into an acceptable shape and keep you from deep breaths. God forbid you should stop holding your belly in. It's sloppy, and once you begin, who knows where it will take you. Sloppy wasn't a thing you could be in my family but my mom got heavy, and my dad turned on her. It showed that you had no discipline, no will. You were letting things go that you should stay on top of for the good of the family. The governess says: Get in gear. Suck it up. Carry on.

I think the governess might be English, which coincidentally my mother was, too.

The antidote to the governess is a kind of spiritual dialysis. Going for a bike ride would probably be the best possible protocol, what with all that beauty passing by and the wind blowing your ears back like a spaniel's, but any escape into nature works. So does singing loudly to the radio or eating caramel corn. In an office setting, you can daydream. Picture warm coastal waters with sea turtles gathered near the rocks. Picture sleeping under the stars. Imagine the mean boss onstage in underwear, or the aggressively chatty coworker suddenly able to mouth only silent goldfish words. In the opening created by distracting the governess, life becomes theater, of both the absurd and the poignant all around us. Free from her grim gaze, you observe the new poppies or the father whose kid has a brain tumor who wears crazy gorgeous socks to match his formal ties. You notice Elizabeth Warren refusing to shut up on the Senate floor while reading the letter of Coretta Scott King, even though the majority leader tells her to stop, repeatedly.

Scary thoughts floated by in my mind, but so did ribbons of hope, and the knowledge that we have an amazing vet who would never let anything bad happen to Lady Bird, even if at some point she couldn't save her life. You make the plan but you don't plan the result, so I would do whatever further tests or procedures the vet might recommend and try to keep the patient—me—comfortable.

The governess slid her glasses to the end of her nose and peered down at me sternly. She said that that was very nice indeed but we needed to hope for the best and prepare for the worst.

Good girl that I am, I obeyed. I imagined holding Lady Bird while she was being euthanized. . . . But then I laughed, gently, out of the blue. What a silly person I can be. Laughing is the breeziest breeze of them all; laughter is grace exhaling bubbly breath.

When I entered the vet's office a couple of hours later, she was standing there with tears in her eyes, because she loves my dog so much and had good news. She had not found anything wrong with her—no masses in any of her major organs, not bad cancers, not even good treatable cancers that I might have settled for, just some dumb stupid old-age things like the ones I have. She said we should retest Lady Bird in a few months. I said, "Well, sure, that works." Relief blew away all fear.

Outside, as I held the car door for Lady Bird, a soft breeze stirred somewhere stage left, a mercy of cool that might just temper the heat.

Seven

✦

CAN YOU LOVE ME NOW?

✦

I have a doctorate in morbid reflection, and a grave anxiety disorder, which is not ideal for our times as we join hands to turn climate change around. Maybe the young, our grown children, who can be a bit tense and self-righteous about the whole situation, would prefer we step out of the way, after the mess we've made, but we can help. I try to keep pointing out flickers of light, hope, and love all around, to stand in witness to the times we have come through after shame and hopelessness nearly did us in. We changed the world through mass mobilization, disruption, and singing loud songs of protest and equality, followed by organizing and smart work on the inside by those committed to change. The young should not be mean to us, because our hearts are good and we are trying to get them a decent government. We show up for marches even as our feet hurt. We know things: how to write grants, draft new laws, organize at the grassroots level. We are not only useful, but formidable, if creaky and tired, and we know all of the words to the great protest songs.

We are sorry that we're handing off an earth in crisis, but we still have much to give. Our generation of scientists has amassed the greatest climate and energy data possible for the young to build on. We know some truths, via the poets and great spiritual masters on whom we cut our seekers' teeth. We know one overarching truth: that all things are covered by the Serenity Prayer. We've been sunk; we've risen. We know some movies that will change you. We can help the young to remember to keep looking up with fascination at the wonders and weirdness of this earthly amusement park. Plus, we have money.

We can be good at approaching life with perspective. My husband says that ninety percent of what is beautiful, meaningful, and useful in the world is visible in a ten-minute walk.

I love this, but it doesn't always ring true, what with my PhD in morbid reflection.

Neal also has a number of theories that are a

bit of a stretch for me, namely the minimal organizing principle—that because the world keeps
reorganizing itself, generation after generation,
after Hitler and the Iron Curtain and custody bat-
tles, we can live in trust that the world keeps picking itself and us up. We cry out, "But this time it's
totally hopeless," whether the catastrophe is the
pandemic, nuclear arms race, the rise of fascistic
governments, or the hateful mother of our most
beloved young relative, and the world nods gently—
it really understands—picks us up, holds us, feeds
us. Neal believes it will again, that it always does,
that this is life's nature.

I sometimes try to badger him into defending
his theory in light of climate change, and get him
to see that we must stop traveling and get Teslas or
stop driving, but we can't afford Teslas and he
doesn't agree that we need one. He likes the old
cars we have. We fell in love in my Subaru, and
last week he whisked me away on the white horse
of his minuscule Chevy when I was having a melt-
down in public.

Putting aside the fact that fossil fuels have
destroyed the world, cars have meant freedom
and intimacy since I first got my learner's permit
fifty years ago. (That can't be right.) Sorry about

the melting permafrost, but cars can be mobile churches or mosques. You are pointed in the same direction with someone you trust, with sacred music on, Bach or Springsteen, and you end up somewhere you wanted or needed to be, sharing epiphanies or life-giving gossip. We are sick about the polar bears, but be honest, cars are why anything about life works at all.

When I met Neal in 2016, we might not have had a second date had it not been for my car. (When the initial audition was over and I had to leave to drive across the county on an errand, he asked if he could come along, so we had a second hour, and a third, where we jammed, laughed, sneaked sideways glances at each other. I saw high intelligence in his eyes, and large, beautiful hands. We had the Beatles station on.) In a car, you're taking turns sharing the podcasts of your life. You see beauty passing outside the windows, while the scary aspects—i.e., other people—can't get to you, unless you get carjacked. No salespeople or relatives. But horribly, at some point, you have to get out of the car.

One recent hot summer night, we got out a block away from a great old Art Deco theater in Berkeley. We were there to see a cherished friend of mine perform onstage with a storytelling guild. Neal had heard the guild before and said I would love the guild's lively hostess, the emcee. My friend had said she and three or four others each had ten minutes or so to tell a story about their childhoods in Berkeley.

She sort of glossed over the "or so" part, and the "three or four others." But I had shown up because I am a good friend and secretly believe that God loves us more for good deeds—although the awful truth, as I understand it, is that God simply loves, period.

I'd like to know if God gives us points for showing up or simply marks us present.

I don't love these sorts of performances, or readings, for that matter, when writers and poets go on twice as long as they're supposed to. I feel like a hostage. Twenty-five minutes of poetry and I think of chewing my arm off to get out of the trap. This week, so much was going on. I had been tangling with my son Sam and agonizing over Trump and the constant stirring up of stuff to terrify us. But I was so excited about my friend's debut.

Neal really loves live performance. (Also, very old black-and-white movies, and extended baritone sax solos. Eeesh.) He said we would leave right after my friend performed. But when we met up with her before the show began, she said she had to go last, and then added guiltily, of six. In the second half. After an intermission.

For some reason, this filled me with something close to terror, an ancient archaeological anxiety that I remember having as a young girl. It's as if all that fear I had in first grade, and all the gum and watermelon seeds and cherry pits and school paste I ate then never completely left, instead transforming into a big seed in my tummy that over six decades has been activated by extreme stress every so often. It glows with misery deep inside.

And so I was not at my best when the hostess took the stage. Neal clapped, nudged me, whispered, "There she is." Yay. Let the show begin.

She looked and sounded like a lot of fun, which I don't like in a person. I hated her. I hated her voice and her dress. The perdition of junior high flashed before my eyes: she was the popular girl from eighth grade, a phony in beautiful clothes, a cheerleader to the wired dork I had been. I knew that I was being an asshole, that I was irrationally scared, and I felt trapped.

Her intro to the evening took fourteen and a half minutes. Everyone laughed at her inane jokes. To compensate, I studied the magisterial theater: it made you feel like you were supposed to be doing something important. She said there would be six storytellers, with a fifteen-minute time limit for each. I clenched my teeth, clenched everything that clenches, and maybe a couple of areas that are not meant to. And more good news! At intermission, she was going to offer audience members three minutes onstage each to tell their stories of childhood in Berkeley.

This was when panic rose in me. Three minutes? They'd each need a minute to get onstage, another for an intro, applause, an exit. Pressure began amassing in me like steam. How close to the surface all that deep, confused sadness is! I leaned over and whispered to Neal, "She is everything I hate about life."

He looked at me, puzzled. Really? Letting people know you too well is like the commercial for a telephone company with the hapless person trying to find decent reception: "Can you hear me now?" Our bitter, hard, screwed-up places spool out over time in a marriage or intimate relationship. Our crazy inside-person shows.

Yes, I'm odd, endlessly judgmental, secretly antisocial. Can you love me now?

Lockjaw set in and my eyes stopped blinking, but the lights were low enough so no one but Neal could see. The mango seed of anxiety and school paste glowed inside me. I imagined army-crawling to the car and texting Neal from there to come meet me. But he had the keys.

The first person got up, a young man in full punk. He had an odd, vague affect and jerky unhinged movements, like a marionette trying to be somewhere else. He spoke in a fitful manner and couldn't seem to seize on what he was trying to say, as he rummaged through the notes in his head, which didn't exactly make any sense. On and on he went, and inside me, the ticker was going and ten minutes had come and gone and then another ten minutes passed and he was still rambling. I suddenly wondered if I had just screamed out loud and people around me were shocked but trying to be polite.

My mind felt out of control. I couldn't find my center, the base camp, and a mean voice narrated the disaster of me. My stomach filled with acid, and I remembered that a caterpillar inside the chrysalis digests itself by releasing enzymes that dissolve its tissue, so only the specified cells that will eventually become eyes, wings, a mouth remain. I've read that if you cut into a cocoon at a certain stage, you get butterfly soup, which was what I was beginning to feel like.

The first person, as it turned out, was by no means the worst. The hostess reappeared to lead the audience in applause, segueing into a lengthy introduction of the second person, Matron Barbie. She opened her mouth and out came vague sludge, with her pedigree, street addresses, and a recipe, but no shape and no end.

I began to blink back tears. I was a panicky eight-year-old again. Why this extreme reaction? Who knows? Besides, "Why?" is rarely a useful question. Yet for some reason this hit on everything in my childhood, what an odd misfit I'd always felt like, racked with impostor guilt and hostage syndrome, worried that I might be insane and people might find out. That had not happened for a while. Something here, in this theater, had opened the vein of panic.

I managed to get through Matron Barbie. It helped that I could tell by Neal's body language— squirming and dropping his head back—that he was not enjoying it, either. An hour had passed. The evening was out of control. I once read a report that when asked, people guessed they had eighty percent control of their days—schedules, delays, changes, meetings, traffic, reception, et cetera, but that in reality, it was only three to seven percent. Yet most of my life force goes into trying to self-will life and me into cooperating with how I think things should be. Awareness of this can be funny if you are not having a break-down in a public setting. If you are, then not so much.

It occurred to me that maybe this was a fun-house mirror. I speak on stages to people like those who were in this theater. They always ap-plaud and say nice things. Was everyone here just pretending to enjoy the dreck? Do I sound this self-important to others? Do I trigger the PTSD of the more sensitive audience members, the nuttier ones, like me?

Three-to-seven-percent control means we are mostly at the mercy of chance and mood. My friend Janine, one of whose children is terminally ill, told me about being on a ride at the Santa Cruz boardwalk when her three children were young. They were in tiny cars, Janine furiously and re-sentfully steering to avoid hazardous and incon-siderate drivers, when her husband tapped her on the shoulder and said, "Your steering wheel doesn't actually steer."

Neal clapped for the matron but smiled too enthusiastically. I turned on him. Our marriage was a travesty of incompatibility—extended baritone sax solos! I fumed. Then I couldn't help it, and I whispered, "Are you serious?" It's so wrong that Protestants can't get annulments.

After a long, enthusiastic introduction, the third speaker slunk onto the stage, arrogant as a camel, heavy-lidded with entitlement. He took a leisurely five minutes for desultory witticisms before he got to his childhood in Berkeley. He made the first two speakers seem like Spalding Gray. I imagined stabbing him to death. When somebody's droning at you, your breath gets constricted, as when you're swimming in a dream, your arms become concrete blocks, and it's life or death, and you think scared and scary thoughts.

Bad performance turns you into a would-be sniper, not with a bullet but with a Nerf gun. Just make it stop! I remembered a tattoo on a stranger's arm, the entire secret of life: "It's not them." It's not them making you pissy. But how could it be dear, prayerful me?

I prayed to be restored to ordinary boredom. I studied the baroque chandeliers and decorations. But when tears sprang to my eyes, I had no recourse but to start tapping.

Therapeutic tapping is a form of psychological acupuncture, an alternative technique to relieve stress and anxiety, with a focus on Chinese medicine meridian points. To fully tap each meridian—crown, brow, eyes, chin, chest—makes you look like Rafael Nadal preparing to serve. But there is a short form, tapping the webbing between first finger and thumb. A therapist taught me this, and sometimes it works. Neal finds it hilarious.

I sat in the dark, clapping when other people clapped, trying to pass as a normal person, but still in lockjaw, blinking back tears, doing Lamaze, and now tapping.

The third story went on and on. The seasons changed, my hair turned white, and still I tapped. I was so alone and fragile. I'd gotten into a situation that was supposed to be fun but had turned out to be toxic, and I had no defenses. I'd shown up with loving eagerness. By the end of the third person's story, I was in some sort of fugue state.

Neal peered at me, tilting his head in the universal gesture of "What's going on?" I threw my hands up at him, slightly peevishly, as if he ought to know without asking.

When people know you too well, they eventually see your damage, your weirdness, carelessness, and mean streak. They see how ordinary you are after all, that whatever it was that distinguished you in the beginning is the least of who you actually are. This will turn out to be the greatest gift we can offer another person: letting them see, every so often, beneath all the trappings and pretense to the truth of us.

But can you love me now?

In addition to the dark impulses and less lovely attributes, the cranky self-obsession, the knowledge of where our bald spots are and the rubbery Jell-O consistency of the tummy roll, our partners see the slippage of our minds, the pockets of butterfly soup—constantly lost keys and phones, and sentences dribbling off into the ether.

You can still love me *now*? Really? Does my family slip you a little something every month?

When intermission began, Neal apologized for the terrible stories we had had to sit through, now almost ninety minutes in. I whispered, "I'm not okay, I feel like I'm having a breakdown." He asked gently what was going on, and I said I didn't know, but I felt like I might be losing my mind. I secretly wondered if I should go to the hospital. Neal looked into my face and I looked back bravely. He asked if I wanted to leave, but I insisted I would be okay in a minute. Right then my friend's oldest friend in the world came up, and we hugged, and she began chatting me up. It helped! She talked about what a fun night it was, and I beamed. What a fraud I am. Can you love me now?

Then my friend's friend's *tenant* popped up, like on *Laugh-In* or a jack-in-the-box. It was a nightmare until she mentioned that today was her tenth sobriety birthday.

Wait, what? Wow. Another nutty alkie in recovery. Thank you, Jesus. It was like hearing someone speak English at a train station in Siberia. I got to make a fuss over her. Such comfort to get out of myself, the first pleasant moment in the past ninety minutes.

She said she needed fresh air, and I tagged along, out into the warm night, and I blurted out how crazy I felt, how bad I thought the stories were, because I do know that the movement of grace in our lives so often begins with desperation and blurt. I was near tears. I starting tapping again, to keep from spinning out into the cosmos.

Smiling faintly, the woman said, "Are you *tap-ping*?" Uh-oh; busted.

I said, "I feel very strange, almost like I'm having a bad trip."

She nodded. "Boy, do I know the feeling. Listen, I'm an acupuncturist, and I have all my clients tapping."

We laughed. Something inside gave a little, unclenched a bit. My Sherpa had arrived. There's a recovery story of a man whose small plane goes down in the tundra. He wakes up in the hospital with a cast, pissed off. A nurse asks why, as she thinks his rescue was a miracle, and he says, "I lay in my plane overnight, broken, freezing, praying to God to save me. What a joke." The nurse points out that's he's alive, and safe, and he says bitterly, "Yeah, because some Sherpa came along."

My Sherpa asked, "Would you give me your hand? Let me do it for you." And she tapped me on the webbing of one hand, tapped me back to my body, which brought me back to my life, which right then seemed sweetly timeless, so different from the quicksand time of the agonizing stories. Then she took my other hand and tapped, like a staccato laying on of hands.

Soon the lobby lights blinked off and on. Once

more into the breach! Somehow space and time
and the release of panic made it possible for me to
go back in and sit beside Neal through another
absolutely crazy hour of agonizing patter and stories. I imagined presenting my case at the com-
mitment hearing: Where was the fifteen minute
deadline, Your Honor? Absolutely nowhere. Where
was any kind of craft or preparation? I rest my
case. The Buddhists ask, "Would you rather be
right or happy?" and I just want to say that in this
case, I was right, objectively. I kept tapping until
Neal took my hand, as he shook his head at the
fourth storyteller's rambling account of Berkeley
High in the eighties. But by now I believed that at
some point the night would end, and it crossed my
mind that soon I'd be cocooned in the car with my
person, imitating everyone meanly, which can be
salvation.

Well, I was wrong, as the night was not going
to end, ever. Entire seasons passed. I felt cataracts
growing in both eyes. But at least I wasn't butterfly soup anymore, and that was a small miracle.
I also remembered we had a jar of macadamia
nuts in the car—like salty, buttery Prozac—and
the Beatles station, the most magical music that
has played our whole lives. Reasons to live! Oh,

and Neal. I breathed that in and out, in and out: the "Oh, and Neal" part.

My friend finally appeared onstage, an apparition, a beloved sister, a larger Audrey Hepburn type in black capris and a classic white blouse. She told us of her first teenage kiss, at the Berkeley Botanical Garden in the Oakland Hills, which transported me to those lovely acres that hold every California plant and terrain, bluebells and redwoods and cacti, colors and flavors and shapes from everywhere, diverse as Oakland. I savored memories of slow nature walks through its paths and hills, the blend of science and creativity, which save us.

We sang along to the Beatles as we drove home across the bridge, and no one could have ever guessed how afraid I had been earlier. So to the younger people who have such fear about the future, I would say that older people have a lot of fear, too, but we know things. Fear is not facts. We have seen life self-correct again and again. Stick around, and against all odds, you will, too. We know that science and love almost always win the day, honest to God. We will march with you, mad and afraid, and help cause a holy commotion, and we will be singing.

Eight

+

FOUR NIGHTS, THREE DAYS

+

M y comedian friend Duncan Trussel once said nine words onstage that changed me. He said that when you first meet him, you're meeting his bodyguard. I wrote it down and later taped it to my bathroom mirror, where all truth resides at least briefly. His bodyguard is smart and charming, and keeps people out. Deep inside, his true self is very human, which is to say beautiful and kind of a mess— needy, insecure, judgmental, like most of us. It is full of love, warmth, and rage. Duncan is devoted to his Neo-Hindu spiritual community. Their guru says to love and serve and feed everyone: forty years ago he cofounded a medical organization that has restored eyesight to millions of people around the world. So Duncan feeds and serves everyone he can through this community, and he

is also acerbic, and often on edge, having survived cancer in his thirties, and then having had
a child last year. We share the belief that we are
both loving awareness with skin on, and walking
personality disorders. We believe in deeper reali-
ties of stillness and magic. We see the earth as
forgiveness college, and recognize that we are at
best B–/C+ students. We believe in the immortal-
ity of the soul, although he finds it hilarious that
I am a Christian, and I think it is hilarious that he
is whatever the hell he is. When troubles befall,
we are both combo platters of anxiety, faith, con-
striction, sharing, expansion, trust, and panic. He
loves, judges, forgives, and grouses, gives and re-
ceives deep love, shares life's inevitable pain, and
maintains his humor and belief that love is who
we are and why we are here.

Me? Well, of course, I believed this, too, until
the power went out in our county for four days,
and I spiraled into victimized self-righteousness.
And it was good.

Pacific Gas and Electric is a privately owned
utility whose outdated equipment starts catastrophic fires in California's glorious forests.
Once it has started a fire, PG&E turns off our
power to prevent the fire from spreading. At the

time the fire was two counties away, but forecast-
ers were predicting what they were calling a "historic wind event." While we all have tiny opinions
on PG&E, we sprang into action, grumpy but prepared. Some of us bought generators. Most people
bought firewood, non-perishable food, and bat-
teries. We rose to the occasion.

Everyone was there for everyone else, the
first day.

Neal took our best space heater to an invalid
who had a small generator. We invited our beloved friend Maya to stay with us in the spare
room. She is twenty years younger than we are,
lives in the boonies, and had recently separated
from a neurotic narcissist named Erik. He is much
older, has money, has been unfaithful, and almost
worst of all, is boring. We helped her settle in and
did not add to her narrative of what a pathetic,
unworthy shit he was. We nodded, plugged her
lamp into a socket in our generator, got her extra
blankets and a random cat.

We discovered early on the first day of the
power outage the great lesson of life, which is how
much actually *does* work all the time: candles,
water, soap, pets, walking, friends. And gas! We
had hot water. We had a laugh about what whiny

babies we were, and reminded one another how, after each blackout, we're actively grateful for all the blessings of our lives, for about twenty-four hours.

The Wi-Fi didn't work, and periodically not even the phone, but man, indoor plumbing did, which is the beginning and end of all civilization. I savored the hot shower. To show my inside person that there was a caring mother on deck, I lovingly washed my big funny body, my baby belly button, behind my ears, between my toes, as I had for my baby son, and his. I put on a pretty shirt, forgiving pants, excessive mascara. I partook of saltines with peanut butter and raspberry jam, and then a fistful of Good & Plenty: heaven.

The sky was a bowl of arctic blue, with a touch of aqua, and sun dappled the sidewalks through our trees. Shadow steals the show so often, when light isn't looking. Light thinks it is Beyoncé, shimmying with celestial meaning, but shadow knows that without it, we ain't got nothing to show for ourselves—no paintings, poetry, or song.

I loved that we could use lamps and the microwave, but the generator sounded like a jet engine and some of the generator-less neighbors seemed distant and maybe bitter. Neal and I walked into town to survey the unplugged scene and bask in community love. At that point, I still liked him very much, partly because he had bought and set up the generator, which meant that while half the neighbors hated me, I would have milk for my coffee.

We walked along with espresso in paper cups, and five minutes later, I had an epiphany: I had appreciated the first sip greatly, one of my favorite tastes and pleasures, but that was the last I'd really noticed it. And now it was gone. What part of each day do I do this? I'm guessing about two-thirds.

Everyone I know cleaned a bad kitchen or bedside drawer that first day. That morning I got a text from Duncan in Los Angeles: "Try not to catch on fire today."

The bad voice inside me cried, "What if, what if?" What if the power stays off, or this happens every month? But the gentle voice of the mother who had cleaned between my toes said, "What is? What is?" "What is" was food, nature, one another, what we have and what works.

Later, antsy with the lack of internet, I took an orchid to a dying relative, a rose to a friend with testicular cancer (the same cancer Duncan survived in his thirties). I brought pumpkins to a shut-in mother so her three wild-gorilla children could make jack-o'-lanterns. My calling is to be a missionary; but I was not upset to bask at the same time in political news on the radio, junkie that I am, and the car was warm. Shadow and light, mobile division.

Almost every traffic light in the county was out. Signs said that intersections were now all four-way stops. Everyone practiced You go, I go, waving hello. After you, my dear Alphonse. Sometimes the movement of grace looks like letting other people go first.

Maya was in and out all day, sometimes teary and other times fierce in her conviction that the blackout was a kind of punctuation. She visited a girlfriend and came back refreshed, got on the phone with horrible Erik for a while, and cried behind her closed door. We turned off the generator at eight, so the kids next door could sleep. The world was instantly a better place without that godawful roar. We read by the light of electric lanterns.

The next day was Sunday. We woke up and looked out the window at the trees in perfect stillness. Hah, we said; some historic wind event. The sun was coming up redder than usual because of the smoke from the neighboring fires. The joy of light: you can see, and read! It bathes you in radiance, and you don't stumble over things, which can make you feel stupid. Illumination is a stand-in for positive spiritual experience. We take it for granted until it's snatched from us, which is pretty much the sum of human experience. Snatch, mourn, restore, appreciate, snatch.

I tried to convince Neal and Maya to go to church with me. But Neal needed to go to the church of his garden, and Maya said she had a deadline. I think she wanted to be near her phone in case Erik called, which he did as I headed toward the front door. She was cooing in a slightly injured way by the time I turned the knob. In recovery, they say there are no victims, only volunteers, and in this case it was true.

St. Andrew was beautiful by candlelight. With no electric lights or microphone, the service was infinitely and beautifully primitive. It reminded me of Aboriginal ceremonies I have seen in movies, the people close to the earth, to vibrations, songlines, the ancestors. How have we lost that connection? It is partly that there is so much goddamn data, streaming endlessly. I often choose the metallic chilling stream of toxic information. People in the desert do the stream of life, the constellations, their hearts, dreams, each other. My dear Jesus shares this quality, plugged into something both spirit and earth, life as gorgeous and hard, shimmering and dark. I am plugged in, too, sometimes. And I do rejoice and feel glad, especially when I am warmer and have Wi-Fi.

The fifteen of us in the sanctuary were all wearing parkas and were joyous, singing, praying, passing the peace, until, horribly, our interim pastor began her sermon. She is my age, African American, and someone had ratted me out to her. Someone had told her my heart was hard toward Erik.

"How can we live in faithfulness and freedom when we're in judgment?" she began. "How do we not become a part of the problem? Who is not qualified to inherit the kingdom of God, according to me?" she asked. "To judge is human, and the mystery of faith is that you are forgiven for judging even before you judge."

However, she went on to say that the closed heart of judgment destroys your life, so that's not ideal. Focusing intently on what the judged per-

son was doing, or not doing, robs only us. Obsession robs us of freedom, awareness, a sense of
life's sweetness. I heard the pastor say that God
was big enough to handle both Erik and me. Let
God deal with the greedy, stingy, disloyal. We
could advocate for public school teachers, for the
poor, for public utilities. "Or," she added, "you
could go for a walk."

So after the service I went for a walk. Part of
me wanted to avoid hearing about Maya getting
back together with Erik. Part of me wanted God as
the Great Outdoors. The historic wind event had
not begun, but there were uprooted trees from
over the years beside the trail. I didn't hear many
birds. I wondered if the smoke had driven them
inside.

I ambled. When there is nowhere to go, you
realize that most of the time you are racing pur-
posefully from place to place, missing out on how
wondrous it all is, even the upended trees. They
are animate, even though they are no longer alive
and growing. They give off such life force.

One massive redwood was decapitated, pulled
out of its space, with all but its roots and a few feet
of three-foot-wide trunk left. I stopped. It was the
underneath made visible—what you never notice

when you're racing around is this complex, vibrant, breathing reality all around us. We walk right on by, or we sum it up efficiently: Ah, yes, I see it, I know what it is. I've seen it before. Very nice. Next!

But tree roots show us that there is a massive, sturdy, and ethereal connection underneath us, not just dirt or the vacuumy emptiness of the abyss. So I rooted myself right then and there in my body, felt my feet on the earth, felt held.

The earth is faith. It will hold. Rooting ourselves in the earth that supports us leads to our being rooted in the faith that we are not alone, that we are connected to all of this, to the fabulous humus underneath us, the nourishment of our best if paltry love.

All of this enlightenment made me very hungry. I started to head back home, but I paused a moment longer with the roots, the network and pattern in the tangle. The exposed root ball was witchy, as if it could come creeping after you, reaching for you. It looked like a mess, as if the tree had been standing on a snarl, yet it had held up the tree, helped the tree get what it needed to live, which is earth, air, sky. Such great industry under the earth on which we stand. Someone is paying attention while we flit about and check our texts. Something speaks to the plant, to release its pine cones' seeds: Let it rip. Or: At ease, Sergeant, hold on to those seeds for a more auspicious season. Something speaks to me through Neal and my very closest people. They speak plant.

When we woke on the third day, the historic wind event was in full force. Thank God that PG&E had turned off the power lines. But still: Oh no, wind! I'm sorry, but there is not much good about the wind. It lashes and pricks you, plus it fucks up your hair.

Neal and I took the dogs for a walk, my big, perfect Lady Bird, my son's crazy and loud little terrier. We tried to get Maya to come with us, but she was on the phone with Erik. I wanted to tell her that when you break up with someone, the main thing is to keep that person's worst qualities to yourself for when you get back together.

I tried to feel like I was one with the spirit of the gale, the fierce and magnificent force of the earth, but then sand flew into my eyes and I could feel my skin get blotchy, and Neal had begun to annoy me.

There is one area in which Neal and I so disagree that whenever he brings it up, I realize we are really poorly matched, that we should end this horrible experiment and save ourselves a lot of pain. It is on the subject of suffering. He believes it is always a blessing and a portal. I believe it is sometimes these, but I find his view elitist. He has the luxury to see it this way. He manages to shoehorn it into conversation from time to time—some gremlin or personality flaw causes him to voice it—and then he wants me to debate. Most of the time I let it go and refuse to participate. But what with the wind pricking at me, I couldn't handle it. My bodyguard stepped in and said to Neal, "Stop."

He looked surprised and aggrieved, as he does every time I make it clear I don't want to debate. He started to explain his position, trying to get me to engage. I secretly shut my heart to him completely. I forgot that this hurts only me.

I could not get home fast enough so I could be alone again, all but humming happy songs while imagining turning to Neal and lighting into him about his need to win arguments.

And then I had an insight.

I realized that the bodyguard of which Duncan speaks protects other people from *me*, from my saying what I honestly think about them and their decisions. But the bodyguard also protects me from me, both from seeing how damaged my mind is, how terrified and angry and shut down—coincidentally, a bit like my parents' minds—and from letting too much of my loveliness show.

I let this revelation sink in swampily. By the time we got home, I was kittening up to Neal, stroking his back, resting my head against his shoulder, all but purring. I told him I was sorry for our stupid argument.

Then I lied.

I said I had to leave right away and meet up with a woman in my recovery community, an older friend named Caroline with whom I can share everything. I said we had a date at noon.

I called Caroline retroactively from the car and begged her to meet me somewhere. She said we could meet briefly in her car at a certain beautiful overlook nearby. I knew that this was a trick: she was going to get me to see the view, to realize we live in the most beautiful place on earth and maybe, just maybe, we could dig it, rejoice, and be glad in it.

Well, I wasn't going to fall for that old scam.

At the overlook in her car, facing our mountain and the canyon, I told her all: how benevolently

I had worked through the tiff with Neal, and, in passing, his bad diet, which has caused me to gain weight, and my malice toward Erik, and my ensuing distance from Maya.

Caroline listened with her eyes closed. Typically she might bring up my minor control issues, and how my feelings about men predate my having met Neal or Erik by six or so decades. But this time, when she opened her eyes, she said, rather gently, that God's love is not the same as human love. My love, she said, is fraught with conditions, delusion, and judgment.

Fraught? She was saying my deep and loyal love was *fraught?*

She added that if I am in service to love, to all that is lovely, I might allow this other love to flow through me and direct it to the offender. And the only offender was me.

My bodyguard was flinching but did not pull out its pepper spray, as I already knew this fact to be true. Duncan's group swears by the belief that everyone, no matter how seemingly vile, is secretly God in drag, and I usually believe this. But really? Erik? And me?

Then she looked out of the car and sighed. I knew what was coming. "Wow," she said, her gaze

lifted to the mountain. "We live in such a beautiful place. . . ."

When Neal and I woke at dawn on day four,
I had a fleeting sense of connection to
much of what I had seen and been through, to the
cold and warmth, the roots and the sky, the view
from above and the peanut butter saltines.

Now all I had to do was hunt it down and wres-
tle it into a cage or a Word doc.

There were rumors of returned power in our
county's northernmost towns, and we got a text
from the police department that we would all have
power sometime that night. Maya decided to go
back to her own house. I made her a snack pack for
the drive, which was only half an hour away, and
offered her my son's dog as a companion, so she
didn't have to go back to Erik. She thought this
was very funny but wouldn't take the dog. Dam-
mit. I didn't actually hate Erik anymore. Duncan
said years ago that when you're with an awful
person, you're not around a villain, you're with a
person who's suffering deeply, starving for love.

We still didn't have Wi-Fi and I had run out

of books on my tablet; if the power came on too late, I'd have to read a real book by lantern. Small print in poor light is hard in older, dimmer age.

So Neal and I headed to the great independent bookstore Book Passage in Corte Madera, which had its power back on because the county hospital is nearby. Book Passage has been passionately loyal to me since my first book came out forty years ago, but my plan was not to buy a large-print book and thus support them. It was to use the store's Wi-Fi to download a book online to read on my tablet. In the café, with tea and ginger cookies and Wi-Fi, we both caught up on the news and Twitter. Then I hunched over my tablet and downloaded a book, like a thief.

And that was the moment I looked up and around, busted by my own conscience.

I got up and went to the Large Print section. I picked out my first large-print thriller, which is like buying a pack of literary Depends, and paid for it at the register. I flirted with the elderly book-seller. The wall around my heart was more porous again. The wall is the bodyguard. When it is soft and porous, there is indeed risk, but at the same time, my essence could stream out like a sprinkler and make contact with the world, with life.

FOUR NIGHTS, THREE DAYS

When the lights go out and we deploy our candles and lanterns, we see the beauty of contrast, which makes both light and shadow precious. In art and photography it is called chiaroscuro, as in scenes of cobbled European streets, or Caravaggio, and of course, we find shadow and light in our families, and ourselves.

When Neal and I got home, our electric power was back on. We binged on TV and Wi-Fi, read in bed for a while, and then celebrated the miracle of having the luxury of turning off the lights. We rested in the dark, hidden away and weightless, free of gravity for a while. Darkness can be so soothing when you know it won't last forever; you can slip into shadow as a refuge, especially when the light has been pitiless. Spiritual wisdom has it that light is the truth, but there are many kinds of beauty in darkness, like the silver-golden glitter in the internal dark when we close our eyes, and at twilight, and at dawn.

Nine

✦

ONE WINGED LOVE

✦

The search for the holy grail has been called off. No grail to find, no code to break. All along, it turns out that there was only the imperfect love of a few trusted people and that in troubled times, like heat waves, epidemics, and blackouts, most people bring their best selves. No ultimate answers, only the blessings of friendship and service; silence and music, the beauty of the seasons and skies, creation, in art and life's phases—birth, death, new life. Sigh.

This is so disappointing.

Love will have to do, along with bright and dim memories, some that still hurt, others that we savor like Life Savers tucked away in our cheeks.

And there are the stories that buoy us up like water wings. My father, raised in Tokyo, gave my brothers and me the books of Japanese fairy tales he had read as a child, "The Tongue-Cut Sparrow," "The Peach Boy," and the one about heroic little One-Inch, the tiny samurai with a sewing-needle sword and a noodle-bowl boat and chopstick oars. My mother read to us from the Brothers Grimm. I did not see myself in the beautiful princesses but instead in the youngest prince in "The Six Swans," the oddity, the one who is not wholly saved from the spell and ends up with one arm and one wing. This is the truth of who I am: weird, beautiful, hobbled, beloved.

The facts of this world will never satisfy the human heart, but what we give each other can, when it holds love. I can touch the truth of me and my hope of salvation in two worthless artifacts my parents left behind. A small ivory elephant that my father got in India when he was a boy, and a rustling corn-husk angel Christmas-tree topper that my mother brought home from Hawaii when her life came crashing down.

My parents' childhood homes were far away, in foreign lands. My father was the son of a missionary minister in Tokyo, Presbyterian—God's frozen chosen—and my mother the daughter of a dockworker in Liverpool. Both were raised by grief-stricken mothers. My paternal grandmother lost her three-year-old daughter, my father's big sister, in Japan to the 1918 flu pandemic. My maternal grandmother was widowed in Liverpool after accidentally having twin girls when she was in her mid-forties. She brought them by steamer to America as nine-year-olds, strangers in a strange land. My father fought the Japanese on Okinawa, young men he might have grown up with. My parents were wired for survival and making good impressions. I know that like all of us they longed for home, the promise of being welcomed and received in love. "If we didn't believe in homecoming, we couldn't bear the day," W. S. Merwin said once on the radio. My parents tried to create this home together, and it was impressive from the outside. Inside? Not so much: two isolated, repressed if gregarious souls doing their inadequate best.

How did my brothers and I learn love from such wired scarcity? How did we learn kindness, trust, and loving fun when not a single one of these was a consistent part of my parents' marriage?

We got it where we could. We got it from my parents' siblings and best friends, who adored us, who were interested in knowing us. We got it from the parents of *our* best friends, who wanted us to come over, who asked good questions and talked about real things. We got it from teachers whose admiration gave us hope in the worst times: hope as the tiniest flicker, but still a flicker. In life's Lost and Found, we saw that flicker in a few odd-balls along the way and we said, "Dibs on you." And we got it from stories.

I got it especially from "The Six Swans," which was one of my mother's cherished fairy tales. Most fairy tales scared me, as most things in life scared me, but I didn't mind this one so much. At least there were no snakes or bones, just violent, jealous wives.

In the Brothers Grimm version, a widowed king gets tricked into marrying the daughter of a witch. The new wife discovers he has hidden his six sons and one daughter from her, for fear she will do harm to them. He visits them too much for his jealous wife's liking, so she finds out where they are and makes six men's shirts—in her spying, she missed the daughter—each with an evil spell in it that turns them into swans, who fly away.

We did not have a stepmother, evil or not, but we had a rough equivalent, which was my father's mistresses. This cast a spell over my brothers and me, which transformed us, but not into swans. More like penguins or ostriches, or humming-birds, who *can* fly but can't walk. In the story, the king's daughter is heartbroken, and she searches the deep woods until she finds her brother swans living in a rude hut. The swans become human for fifteen minutes a night, and when the princess sees this, they give her the secret formula to re-verse the spell: she must sew them all shirts of net-tles and remain perfectly silent for the six years she has to complete this task. Only six years! And net-tles! They are the meanest of plants. We knew them well, because our father often took us hiking on Mount Tamalpais, where a dangling hand might brush against one as we trudged along. The prick is awful, not like a thornbush, but instead sending a charge through you like a thousand needles on the edge of pain and excitement. Then a rash. It's a bad magic spell of a plant.

My father gave us hiking. We couldn't travel, because we didn't have money, but in all his wreckage—a cold Christian upbringing, a war, and a bad marriage—he knew to hike. We scur-ried along behind him on our short legs through cathedrals of redwood groves, like a cross be-tween ducklings and the Seven Dwarfs. Dad was our god. Leonard Cohen's line that there is a crack in everything and that's how the light gets in has become a bit of a cliché, but for me the song's better line begins the chorus: "Ring the bells that still can ring." My parents rang the bells of civil rights, endless meals with close friends, a heart for underdogs (such a beautiful bell), and this passionate love of the outdoors, which has saved me thousands of times over the years.

I hear these bells when I hold the elephant and the corn-husk ornament. Holding these old items makes me less horrified by the new world.

The elephant isn't the only object my father left us. My older brother has a Chinese-made pistol that Dad told him he took off a dead Japanese soldier on Okinawa. It's in John's sock drawer. Dad used to clean it occasionally. My younger brother has my father's imperial Japanese desk, which had been his father's. My grandfather wrote his Christian books on it, my father wrote his nine books on it, I wrote my first ten books on it, and then I gave it to Stevo.

How paltry and blocked our family love was, how narrow the bandwidth of my parents' spiritual lives. My father tried to raise us on a writer's erratic income and didn't ever quite make it, for which my mother never forgave him. So he took a part-time job in the afternoons as a planning consultant, which helped make ends meet, but it's also where he met his longest-term mistress. I was eleven. My brothers and I stopped by his office every day after school for candy money, and we sucked up to the woman he shared an office with. She was everything my mother wasn't: trim, wealthy, beautifully made-up and coiffed, and she drank with him. My older brother was the one who broke it to me that they were in love. It became clear when Dad and the woman began to take business trips together, and the polar tension in our house rose.

My father kept the ivory elephant on his desk, along with a pencil holder I had made in third grade: popcorn kernels glued to an orange juice concentrate can.

My father got the elephant in India when his missionary parents traveled there to save Hindus from their misguided belief in gods of pure love, forgiveness, joy, and new beginnings. Those silly Indians. Off-white, with golden veins of old age, its trunk down, each toenail carved in, five on the front feet, four in the back. The elephant looked gentle and wise, and most important, it was not

charging you. So many other parts of life were—
mean boys, perfectionism, neighborhood dogs.
You rubbed the belly for good luck. The elephant
had ears that might fly, or at any rate extend for
takeoff and landing. We loved him, pudgy and
baggy with wrinkles. I imagined his inside self
stretching to fill that saggy, baggy skin suit when
he went for a long walk or charged. They are huge,
lumbering, yet somehow the beauty of elephants
is majesty. His eyes were tiny, inward, quiet, unlike my mother's scared eyes on us, and the pred-
atorial eyes of men on our small bodies.

We knew the elephant moved mostly in slow
motion, out of necessity and wisdom.

A studious bunch, we knew more about elephants than any of our friends did. Elephants
were communal. They did not run from the bodies of the dead, as our families did.

Elephants are a good religious figure. They
look like they are made of stone, rock, dirt, as if
on a plain or in a desert, rising out of the earth
fully formed, like buttes in New Mexico. Who but
Dr. Seuss could design such a creation? But nature beat him to it. Ponderous, wrinkled, they
are universally revered as wise and beautiful, unlike our human ponderous wrinkled elders. That

would be me. (Maybe we could see our elderly this way, too, if they were just *bigger*; also, if they didn't produce fistfuls of coupons in the express lane.)

The only songs I remember my mom playing at the piano late at night were "Someone to Watch over Me," and "Danny Boy." No one was trying to save her, separating spiky fibers and carding them into threads for a magic shirt. Only she could have saved herself, but she wasn't ready. She did her best to enjoy her kids and friends while basically having to wear a leaden dental X-ray apron of confusion and sorrow.

I know my father could see who was inside my mother when they met in D.C., when she was thin, beautiful, with huge brown eyes, long dark hair, brilliant and sexy. I don't think he even tried to find her again after she had children. Where was he supposed to have learned about unconditional love, from conservative Christians, four years at Yale, four years a soldier? Who besides the poets he worshipped could have taught him that love is supernatural and homely, soars and sags, is oceanic and a shared tangerine?

Love is gentle if sometimes amused warmth for annoying and deeply disappointing people, especially ourselves. My folks did not have this love for themselves, so they could not have it for each other. Each knew where the nuclear buttons were on the other, and they pushed them. But love doesn't deploy.

Love is someone who will draw near when you cry. Crying wasn't for them. The postwar Eisenhower generation didn't cry. Crying showed weakness. I saw my mother cry twice, once when her big brother died and again when Dr. King was killed. I saw my father cry when his best friend of forty years died and when he finally told me how afraid he was to die.

To me, the most valuable love I adopted from my parents was service and charity to strangers, to the lonely and bedraggled. My mother routinely took in strangers and let them stay with us. She brought home some Australians from a campsite whose boat home wasn't leaving for a week. That was the happiest week I remember as a child.

Love is giving away what you have been so freely given, no matter if you have little opinions on the recipients' personal hygiene. Giving away fills the well. My dad took us to vigils outside the walls of San Quentin, twice during executions. He taught writing there to the inmates. Love is not packaged for individual sale. He loved these men and they loved him, in prison where it is loud and smelly and people fling feces at each other. This would be a bit of a stretch for me. The ones who got out stayed in touch with him.

Stepmothers and mothers-in-law were reviled when I was young, but my friends' stepmothers were often unsung heroes. Mothers-in-law were all comedians' main source of jokes, as were large breasts. (These were about it.) And of course, the princess's stepmother in the tale was evil, as was the mother-in-law: the princess married the king of another province, and silently continued to sew her shirts. She paused from time to time to have babies, which the mother-in-law kept snatching away, telling her son that his wife had killed and eaten them, which is apparently very Germanic. The princess couldn't defend herself because to speak would condemn her brothers to lives as swans, and when a third baby disappeared, the king had no choice but to turn his wife over to the law, who condemned her to death. She worked on the shirts in prison, and when the day came for her execution, she still had one arm to finish on the last of the six shirts.

My brothers and I actually longed for a

stepmother, or at least for our parents to split up.
Dad had the perfectly nice mistress with whom he
worked. It was a flawed system and it almost killed
our mother's dreams, but the love of her friends
and her twin sister's family gave her the courage
to do an amazing thing: she began to work as a
paralegal to put herself through law school in her
late forties, quite heavy and with three kids at
home. Then she got her law degree. My father
played the proud husband at her graduation. A
year later, they finally split up, and she moved to
Hawaii to practice law. She started the first wom-
en's law firm in Hawaii—there is still a commem-
orative plaque outside her old office in Honolulu.

She loved the heat after the foggy docks of
Liverpool and San Francisco. She made sensa-
tional new friends. Friends were her great lifelong
gift, as they are mine. But as the Buddhist saying
goes, wherever you go, there you are, and she was
still our deeply neurotic mother. She had taken
our younger brother with her, and this almost
destroyed him at the time—shy to begin with, in
exile, ending up responsible for Mom's emotional
needs. He came back two years later to live with
my father. My mother missed him, but she threw
herself into her family law practice, often working

pro bono, and charging up a storm on home furnishings and trinkets, like the corn-husk Hawaiian angel tree-topper.

Both part of our family's DNA and yet so different: my father's elephant even and smooth, like my father; my mother's angel scratchy, lovely and voodoo at the same time. The angel had a rattled fabric face, smeared lipstick, and incongruously misplaced glitter. Her supposedly festive sash looks like a strip of bacon now. The hair is raffia straw; barrettes keep it out of her eyes. There are wisps that are loose. There are always wisps. That is the nature of life. She wears a crunchy corn-husk skirt. Corn husks are about scarcity. Corn-husk toys and dolls are what kids make when they have nothing else to create with, and yet here was a somehow poignant little lady. It was my talisman of Mom. It releases all the memories of her in Hawaii, giddy at what she called *her* sunsets, in skirts at the beach because she was ashamed of her stout body. It strikes a reverberating note in my psyche; it sends me on a journey. I can hold her, study her, hear the rustle, and feel my mother. It brings me to my mother's relationship to the object—it calmed her and raised her self-esteem to own such quaint beauty. It filled her with tenderness, and holding it can connect me to this tenderness. My mother was so off in real life, in clothes, moods, disordered eating and makeup. But when I release the judgment—and the shoulds—what remains is the love, the dearness . . . and the aggressive offness. (For example, my first sober Christmas, she gave me her cherished autographed copy of a cookbook called *With a Jug of Wine*. Bottoms up!)

Love can bring people out of isolation, get them to take off the Halloween masks they wear, breathing through the slits. But my mother, English to the core, till the last dog died, wouldn't take hers off. She charged more decorations as she went broke. We brought her home and included her in everything. We were so sad for her. Love can be very sad. She had taught us our entire lives that love meant hospitality, which is beautiful, and she taught us to value respectability, which her dockworker family of origin had not had. If you fixate on respectability and prestige, like my mother, you get a knife-and-fork look in your eyes. To my mom, love in its guise of respectability meant elaborate Christmas decorations and fine meals, the bûche de Noël she made us every year, the upscale Christmas cookies she and her friends frantically baked in our kitchen.

To me, love plops in front of the TV with a bowl of popcorn and you.

Love plops and love also flies: At the end of the fairy tale, as the sister was about to be burned at the stake, she looked up from the pyre and saw six swans flying majestically by. She tossed the shirts over them, and immediately their feathers and swan skin fell off and her brothers stood before her; but the youngest, whose shirt was not quite finished, had one arm and one wing—an imperfect human, like the rest of us.

You'll never be able to fly with one arm and one wing, unbalanced and earthbound. But a wing is soft, feathery, warm, and strong over thin bird bones. You could wrap this wing around yourself if it was freezing or if the sun was too hot. One wing sweeping through the air could take people's breath away, especially when the light shines through.

Here is what I know of love: Love is the gas station and the fuel, the air and the water. You might as well give up on keeping the gas cap screwed on tight, keeping love at bay, staying armored or buttressed, because love will get in. It will wear you down. Love is ruthless, whether you notice this or not. Love is Sandy Koufax, Megan

Rapinoe. It will win. It always does, at least in the long term—think Susan B. Anthony, who died before people like me got the vote.

Trust me on this: We are loved out of all sense of proportion. Yikes and hallelujah. Love reveals the beauty of sketchy people like us to ourselves. Love holds up the sacred mirror. Love builds rickety greenhouses for our wilder seeds to grow. Love can be reckless (Jesus is good at this), or meek as my dog, or carry a briefcase. Love is the old man in the park teaching little kids to play the violin: much time spent tuning, the children hearing their way into the key he is playing. My parents heard the key as success, security, moving expeditiously, and living as expected. But love lumbers like an elephant, it naps on top of your chest like a cat. It gooses you, snickers, smooths your hair. Love is being with a person wherever they are, however they are acting. Ugh. (A lot of things seem to come more easily to God.)

But because one-winged love teems and lurches around us, we can always be hopeful, if not effusive. The hope is knowing that this love trumps all, trumps evil, hate, and death. It makes us real, as life slowly sews us our human shirts. We are being shepherded beyond our fears and needs to becoming our actual selves. This sucks and hurts some days, and I frequently do not want it or agree to it. But it persists, like water wearing through a boulder in the river. Hope springs from realizing we are loved, can love, and are love with skin on. Then we are unstoppable. This hope is from a deep, deep place that somehow my parents seeded. Love is not a concept. It's alive and true, a generative and nutritious flickering force that is marbled through life. I can hold it in my hands whenever I remember to, stroke its ivory belly, hear its crunch, its rustle.

CODA:

BIG HEART

Maybe the poet was wrong when he said the center cannot hold. Maybe it can and does hold. Maybe the center paradoxically holds everything, like the gravity well in which our teeny galaxy is held. Terrible losses befall those we love, and yet we are saved again and again by a cocoon of goodwill, evolution, and sweet milky tea. That is plenty of center for me.

For instance, I am sober, loved, grateful, sometimes brave, and wearing dry pants.

This makes Jesus very happy even when He's had a long day, because this was not always the case for me.

Half a lifetime ago, during a storm on the cliffs of the Esalen Institute, the glorious and exclusive retreat center in Big Sur, I nearly wobbled right off a cliff. I had just published my third book, which had been savaged by most reviewers but admired by a man who was involved in Esalen. He got me a free writers-in-residence scholarship. I was both in a messy manic rut and in sorrow, as my dearest friend in Bolinas had moved to another state with her new husband, my father was still extremely dead, I was poor, and everyone hated my book. But this one man offered me a week's respite from my leaky, moldy basket. I did have God and so believed in the movement of grace. Maybe I would hear the exact right words in a workshop, from a spiritual teacher, or during a deep meditation, or conversely, while Sufi dancing. So I packed my shabby bags.

The man from Esalen picked me up at my dilapidated cabin and drove me for three gorgeous hours down the winding Pacific Coast Highway, all hairpin turns and sharp cliffs above the ocean.

Nothing prepared me for the beauty of Esalen, the twin expanses of crashing eternity and the quiet woods. The man introduced me breathlessly to the friendly counterculture personnel as if he were showing Toni Morrison around. I was given a small cabin with its own bathroom, attached to three others at the cliff's edge, overlooking the hot springs and bathhouse, where, fifty vertical feet below, the waves crashed to the shore. Pelicans glided overhead and otters popped to the surface of the water, bobbing around and wrapping themselves in floating seaweed, inviting us in or showing us all how it is done. (It's a Rorschach test. It's all a Rorschach test.)

Hope filled me for the first time in a while. I unpacked. As is so often the case with grace, you could not have gotten to where I now was from where I had been. I put away all my cutest flowing hippie clothes, three bottles of scotch, a carton of Camels, and a baggie of weed, and then I walked just a few dozen yards to the cliffs.

The ocean pulls you magnetically toward itself, and I ended up there many times a day during the week. There was a rocky graduated slope at first, and then a steep drop. You would really have to be careful at night. It was so spectacularly beautiful that you couldn't help thinking about jumping. Surely, I thought, something would catch me in its wings. Exhilaration rose in me, in tandem with weltschmerz, a weariness of the world's and my endless sorrows. So much suffering globally for most of the world's people, and in our own rough fleeting lives. My family basically died when my father passed. He had been the center of our lives, forever, but no more, and we had not found a new center.

What holds when you and your family are walking toward extinction? Only very small things. You hold hands. You tell one another stories of times when you thought the family would collapse or plummet into oblivion but instead it came through. You try to be kind and humble. You whisper words of love.

I had planned on dropping in on some lectures and workshops at Esalen, hiking and doing yoga and eating healthy hippie food, but mostly spending long hours at my portable typewriter, working on a manuscript, beginning anew. It would be spiritual ICU. I would fix myself. What an excellent idea.

I wrote and drank and found solace everywhere I looked, in writing and walks and naps and mealtime conversations about God and spirit and meaning. I carried a notebook and pen in my back pocket and wrote down everything that caught my attention: the words of the teachers, pithy lines over meals, descriptions of the weather to use in my work. I learned a lot about various ways to higher consciousness. I learned that twilight refers to both evening and morning: dawn is the first light before morning, dusk is the light before nightfall. Some mornings I got up early for a group meditation, when the pale gold sun was just rising over the ridge, so bright it made me squint. Who knew such a show was right there every morning? Everyone I encountered believed in some form or another of a great spirit in our center, which was not hard to imagine, as we were surrounded by such evolved and friendly people, over meals, in the hot springs pool on the cliffs. Some parts of the estate were joyous, with dancing or kirtan, which is Hindu call-and-response chanting. Some were as quiet as a rosy desert, where it seems silent until you become aware of the breeze—breath made visible—and the crunch of your footsteps on the earth's floor, and a few ravens. The quiet was surprising and sometimes uncomfortable. And then there was the smashing, crashing ocean below my cabin.

I often stood above the cliffs listening to the sea, as I did back home in Bolinas, infinite spaciousness and a thousand beautiful memories. Most of my family's sacred times were on Mount

Tamalpais, in libraries, or at the beach in Bolinas, where we had a one-room cabin when I was growing up. We Lamotts could get away from us, each of us lost in beauty and rhythms, a great pulse and expansion that other families might have found in church.

At Esalen, I was mildly drunk by dinnertime every night, and while naturally an introvert and hermit, I loved every conversation. There was Native American art on the walls. I had a very reasonable two glasses of wine every night with my dinner companions, and then a couple of glasses of port later as some of us lingered by the fire. I met the couple who were in the cabin next to me, older than I was but not by much, the woman so genuinely sweet and sexy that I thought she must be a fraud, like Mother Mary as played by a Swedish porn star. Her husband was short and hairy, everywhere but his head. I hung out with the personnel who lived at the institute full-time, so that people could see that I was spiritually evolved, not elitist and self-absorbed like the husband and some of the other guests. Then I went back to my room every night and wrote with a bottle beside me.

Wherever you go, there are always going to

be self-righteous people like the hairy husband, holier-than-thou and convinced they are right, and I am like that (but only some of the time). At Esalen that week, there were also many people of intelligence and goodwill. People for the most part were very kind to odd, shy me. They were often with or married to the assholes. Because I already happened to trust in the good news of Jesus's love, I had to love everyone at Esalen, whether they liked it or not, and that one husband did not like it at all. He really would not give me much more than the time of day. Still, I knew I had to love and pray for the most arrogant people there, if possible, knowing Jesus was peering at me over His Ben Franklin glasses.

God has unconditional love for everyone, whereas I tend to fall a bit short in that regard.

I suspect a number of people have noticed this over the years.

Then rain clouds gathered and it stormed the last two days I was there. I liked this. It was good material for my book, it meant I was forced to stay inside, writing during the day, and I could linger at the fire longer after dinner drinking port with the other alcoholics.

On the last night, I staggered back to my room,

wrote and drank for a while, looked over my notes from the workshops, and then went outside. I did not have a raincoat, but as I was now one with all indigenous people, it was fine. Did the Aborigines wear raincoats? I think not.

I headed to the cliffs. It seemed like a good idea at the time.

I came to out of a blackout five or six feet down a sloppy rocky hillside, digging my fingers and feet like crampons into the drenched earth. It took a minute for me to figure out that I was not dreaming, that instead I must have fallen and landed on the steep slope of the cliff above the rocks.

I somehow pulled and dug myself back to the top. When I finally got there, I threw myself face-down onto the muddy level ground, heaving for breath. I lay gasping for a moment, astonished to be alive, shocked, both relieved and mortified.

All I could think was, Thank you, Jesus, and boy, did I need a drink.

So I did what anyone would do in these circumstances: I tried to crawl back to my room along the walkway in the dark. I came to the threshold of my room, rose to my knees, opened the door, and flung myself inside.

Regrettably, it was the wrong room.

The couple inside were naked on the bed, making love by candlelight, until they started shouting, and threw themselves against the wall, pulling up the sheets as if this were an armed robbery. The sexy, affectionate woman and her primate husband gaped at me, the mud ball on all fours on their floor.

"Sorry, sorry, it's Annie," I cried out, attempting to ambulate by bringing my arms upward in big circles like a windmill. It was hard, what with my clothes heavy with mud, so I gave up and tried to get to my feet. The man was shouting for me to get the hell out of their room, and believe me, I wanted to, but my only option was to leave the same way I had entered, on my knees. So I turned my Komodo dragon body back toward the door, and with as much dignity as I could muster, crawled outside.

I sat down on the edge of the walkway to collect myself and pulled off my clothes. I stood naked in the rain, washing the mud off my face and hands and feet. Then—and I love this about myself—I primly folded up my muddy clothes into a neat pile, and after a while went inside my cabin. I put the clothes into the plastic shopping bag I had brought for dirty laundry and took a hot shower.

No harm, no foul.

Did I finish off the scotch later that night? I would like to say no, of course I didn't, but I did. All that adrenaline had sobered me up, and I had a laugh at how things had really gotten away from me. Talk about the best-laid plans.

But I was not laughing at dawn when I woke up. I realized I could have fallen to my death. And also that maybe I had a slight drinking problem.

I thanked God feverishly for His or Her mercy and begged for help. The first great prayer: Help me help me help me.

I was terrified and hungry. The dining room would open for breakfast soon. I took stock. I had been barefoot and my feet were quite scraped up and one big toenail had broken off halfway down the nail bed. People have always told me I have unusually beautiful, delicate feet, essentially or-namental, and it was a good thing that I was not a farmer. But now they would have looked quite at home with a toe tag: the big toe with the broken nail was bruised and slightly swollen. I took the only action I knew to do: I rubbed them with lotion, and then put on my last pair of clean, dry socks. This is the main way I know we take care of the soul, through the skin.

I went in early to breakfast, praying that the couple next door would not be up. Of course there they were, across the room. The woman waved as you would wave to a baby, opening and closing her fingers against her palm, like we were about to play peekaboo. The man looked at me like a reptile. I ate by myself. Sometime later the woman stopped by my table. She did not hand me the 20 Questions of Alcoholics Anonymous or the name of her therapist. She just said, "Hey, hi."

I tried to look rueful yet warm. You can't really pretend you are just fine when someone has seen you in wallowing warthog mode. She looked at me with such kindness that I teared up and prayed frantically for her to leave. She touched my hand, rubbed my knuckles, and then turned to go. To be looked at that way, from someone's heart, can change you molecularly it you are not careful.

I had the room until noon, when the man who had loved my poor savaged book would drive me home. I packed up my clothes and empty bottles and sat there for a while, desolate. There was a painting in the dining room of the Sonoran Desert, a landscape I first saw as desolation until someone had shown me the bones of the earth poking through the sand, the colors hiding within, even somehow a song. The landscape, with all its weird skimpy bounty, connected the artist to the history of his ancestors, an awareness of its beauty and nutrition. I had nothing like this in my life that I could think of. I sat on my bed and cried.

Weeping, I surrendered.

To what, I couldn't have told you, and my getting sober was still a year away, but I crossed some sort of threshold that morning.

After then, by God, a miracle: my curiosity returned. Before I left for home, I needed to see the hillside I'd fallen down.

The rain had stopped. The sky was milky and someone had been busy with subtle cloud textures. A mackerel sky—stippled daubs like fish scales—to my right. On the left a broad scoop swerved to meet it, subtle but virtuosic.

I walked down the wide dirt path to the hot springs pool, right above the beach. It was so beautiful I could barely stand it. I felt a deep attention. The wind was blowing harder as I got closer to the sea. I hunkered down on my haunches and gazed out at the ocean, the endless waves, the spray near the rocks on the shore.

I could see a couple of otters wrapped in kelp. Some others clung to rocks, a few bobbed on the surface like corks, but mostly they were hiding in protected coves. During storms, mother otters swim upwind, so they can nurse their pups on the leisurely trip back. I, too, have always been fed. Sometimes I experience my soul as a kind of mother—an otter, perhaps, or elephant—and other times like a stoned telegraph operator who is always watching, receiving, decoding, translating. She sees the panorama of human events from her chair in my center, the sad news of the old dog's death, the joy of the new baby, the exquisite ordinariness of it all, watchful, breathing, sipping from a paper cup of water. I thought of the warm car of the man who would drive me home, who loved my bad book and me, and the eyes of the woman at breakfast seeing *me*, not the mess of me. I even saw myself rubbing sweet lotion into my poor feet.

I saw the spindrift come off the waves, lacy spray blowing off the cresting surf, drops of water that looked like fine snow, the powder that blows off hills in the wind. Just then, still hunkered down, attentive, amazed, the wind blowing the clouds into new formations, the center held all these hearts beating at the same time, the otters', the ocean's, and mine.

Acknowledgments

Thank you above all to my beloved editor Jake Morrissey and agent Sarah Chalfant at the Wylie Agency.

Huge thanks to my publisher Geoff Kloske at the incomparable Riverhead Books; copyeditor Anna Jardine; Lydia Hirt and Ashley Garland, who get the word out that I am at it again; and Jackie Shost, who keeps everything there on schedule.

My two hilarious Jesuit brothers and sidekicks Fathers Tom Weston and Jim Harbaugh help me both with my religious and spiritual questions, and with living.

Mark Yaconelli, the dearest, funniest Sunday School teacher I know.

My husband and best friends help me find the words to express what I am trying to say and convince me to take out the rest. Thank you, Neal, and Neshama Franklin, Doug Foster, and Janine Reid.

And infinite thanks always to the people of St. Andrew Presbyterian Church SAPC, Marin City, California. Services at 11:00.